A SECOND BOOK
OF RUSSIAN VERSE

By C. M. Bowra

THE HERITAGE OF SYMBOLISM
FROM VIRGIL TO MILTON

A SECOND BOOK OF
RUSSIAN VERSE

*Translated into English by various hands
and edited by*

C. M. BOWRA

LONDON
MACMILLAN & CO. LTD
1948

COPYRIGHT

PRINTED IN GREAT BRITAIN

PREFACE

THIS book is intended to be a kind of sequel to *A Book of Russian Verse* published in 1943. It contains pieces both from a number of poets not there represented, especially among the forerunners and contemporaries of Pushkin and from among poets who have risen to prominence since 1917. It does not claim to be complete or even very representative, though I hope that it will give some idea of the range and variety of Russian poetry in the last hundred and fifty years. Too large a proportion of the versions in this book are my own work, but this was forced on me by my desire to cover certain periods and authors whom other and better translators have not touched. My own versions would be worse than they are but for kind help from Mr. I. Berlin and Dr. S. Rachmilevitsch. I am grateful to the proprietors of *Horizon, Orion,* and *Mandrake* for leave to reprint here poems which have already appeared in their pages, and to Mr. Edmund Arnold and the Salamander Press for leave to anticipate a volume of versions from Pasternak which they intend to publish. It is also a pleasure to record my gratitude to the following authors and publishers for leave to use their works : Mrs. Frances Cornford and Messrs. Faber & Faber, *Poems from the Russian* ; Mrs. Frances Cornford and Penguin Books Ltd., *Russian Review* ; the late Oliver Elton and Messrs. Edward Arnold & Co., *Verses from Pushkin* ; the late Oliver Elton and the Liverpool University Press, *A Sheaf of Papers* ; Sir Cecil Kisch and the Cresset Press, *The Waggon of Life* ; Mr. W. Morison and the Prague Press, *Pushkin's Poems* ; Mr. W. Morison and the Editors of *Review 46* ; Mr. V. Nabokov ; the Oxford University Press, J. S. Phillimore's *Things New and Old* ; Professor V. de S. Pinto and Messrs. Frederick Muller Ltd., *The Road to the West* ; Professor V. de S. Pinto, Mr. R. M. Hewitt, and Mr. Y. Hornstein for poems unpublished or privately printed.

C. M. BOWRA

OXFORD, *February* 21, 1948

CONTENTS

vii

CONTENTS

CONTENTS

CONTENTS

CONTENTS

xi

CONTENTS

INTRODUCTION

It is often said that Russia is a half-way house between Europe and Asia and that much which Western Europeans find mysterious in the Russian character is due to its Asiatic affinities. Yet in Russian poetry these alleged Asiatic elements are almost entirely lacking. We find neither the mystical fatalism nor the greedy sensuality of the East. Even Asiatic subjects are unimportant ; so transformed are they to suit a Russian outlook. Though Ermak conquered Siberia in the sixteenth century, and though both Pushkin and Lermontov found a powerful inspiration in the Caucasus, Russian poetry has never yielded to oriental influences. Its versification, its forms, its themes, its whole manner are essentially European. It falls into the scheme of European poetry and may, in its different stages, be compared with what was written at the same time in France or England or Germany. But though we may look in vain for a distinction in it between Asiatic and European elements, there is another distinction, not often stressed, between elements which are local and indigenous and other elements which belong to a Western European tradition. From the interaction and connections between these rise some of the special qualities of Russian poetry.

The indigenous elements can be seen most clearly in the special part played by folk-song. Whereas in England and Germany folk-song ceased to be a truly living art in the seventeenth century, in Russia it has survived almost into our own time. No doubt this is due partly to the greater degree of illiteracy in the Russian people, but it is no less due to the unfailing Russian love of dance and music and to the important part which these play in village life. When Russian poetry burst into its wonderful spring in the twenties of the nineteenth century, some poets turned to folk-song for their models. They not only felt more at home with it than with the poetry of Western Europe, but saw that it had its own rules and standards and challenged rivalry in its achievements. In an age of patriotic fervour and belief in a national spirit it was inevitable that poets should try to reproduce this ancient art of their country. Where the way had been opened by men like Bogdanovich and Karamzin, others with greater gifts followed with confidence. The result was that in the age of Pushkin Russian folk-song was never far from the minds of most poets. It inspired the graceful art of Delvieg ; it was responsible for all that is best in the work of Koltsov, who falls into the commonplace when he deserts his popular models ; it was known to Pushkin himself, who made use of it in some of his simplest and most natural songs. In the middle and later decades of the nineteenth century it fell into the background, though it was never quite forgotten. In the twentieth century, especially with the Revolution, it came back into favour. It stimulated Gorky to write that poetry which was his first love before he took to the novel. In *The Twelve* Blok used the metres and language of the *chastushka* or popular song for some of his most telling effects, as in the fifth section where the soldiers mockingly make love to the girl Katya. In Esenin folk-song flowered through a man who was himself a peasant and derived his sweet and subtle art from the songs and mythology of the village. Then, as the authorities paid more attention to the educational task of poetry and insisted that it should be in close touch with ordinary life, the folk-song became a model of what poetry ought to be and was adapted conscientiously to the needs of a new age.

Nor is it merely the forms and themes of folk-song which count. No less important is its spirit, its simplicity of outlook, its concentration on quite humble and familiar situations, its lack of embarrassment in speaking of such matters as first love or shameful humiliation, its charming candour and its sweet ease, its irresistible element of song which insists that it must have a tune even in its words. The directness and the sincerity of Pushkin and Lermontov, their wonderful gift for speaking of themselves without any kind of histrionic decoration, their close-ness to the ordinary human heart and their profound, searching interest in it, are all due to the living tradition of folk-song. What Pushkin learned from his nurse or from gipsies, he transformed into consummate art, but he kept the essential qualities of his models. When Lermontov writes a ballad on the battle of Borodino, it is in the heroic manner of the romantic age, but it owes its realism and its economy to his knowledge of what soldiers feel and think. Where the masters set the example, the later poets have followed it, and Russian poetry, with few exceptions, has maintained this simplicity and ease through its varied career. Even the Symbolists felt its appeal, and there are many moments in Balmont and Blok when the high, hieratic manner finds a new strength from its relation to essentially simple forms of art and feeling. The influence of folk-song has been both an inspiration and a corrective to Russian poets. It has shown them the powerful appeal of ordinary emotions and it has taught them that candour is one of the most important elements in a poet's equipment.

At the same time Russian poetry has its Western and European side. If the poets of the eighteenth century owed their forms and their outlook to France, Pushkin and his contemporaries owed more to England and to Germany. The Russians have an uncommon gift for absorbing foreign influences and transforming them to new uses. But the poetry which they write in such conditions is different from that which is based on folk-song. It is more consciously a work of art ; it aims at a fuller and richer expression than folk-song allows ; it uses the metres and the technique which Europeans have used since the rebirth of poetry in the twelfth century, and it extends their range by many ingenious and happy devices ; it exploits many chapters of experience which lie outside the narrow world of folk-song. It is not instinctive song but deliberate art, the voice not of a people but of highly gifted individuals. In its variety and its range it has made Russian poetry one of the richest in modern Europe. Each generation has taken something from the West and adapted it to some essentially Russian purpose. If Pushkin and Lermontov interpreted the romantic desire for escape and for a full realisation of the human personality, they did so with a peculiar power because they felt this desire strong in themselves and could not gainsay it. If Tyutchev and Fet limited themselves to a highly refined art, as did some of their contemporaries in France, they made it the vehicle of unusual and powerful feelings. If the Symbolists, and especially Blok, believed in a world beyond the senses which can be interpreted only through hint and symbol, the world in which they believed was different from the Ideal Beauty of Baudelaire and Mallarmé and had a close relation to the visionary ideals of Russian mystics. If the Futurists, Khlebnikov and Mayakovsky, owed something in their beginnings to the anarchic violence of the Italian Marinetti, their actual work has no relation to his and speaks far more forcibly from the heart. At each stage the Western influence has been absorbed and transformed and extended.

Though each of these two elements, the indigenous and the

Western, has made its special contribution to Russian poetry, it might be claimed that the most notable Russian triumphs have been gained not through a full exploitation of one or the other of them but through a happy combination of both. The exponents of folk-song like Delvieg have indeed many charming moments, but we miss in them the power and the control which come from the West, and the finest contribution of folk-song is to be seen rather in those poets who used it but passed beyond it to richer and more impressive results. Conversely, the purely Western poets, like Fet or Balmont, seem to move in an atmosphere too rarefied to reflect the full ardours and agonies of the Russian soul. Their delicate and graceful art has not the strength or the appeal which belongs to other poets, like Tyutchev or Blok, who shared their ideals and yet related them closely to Russian life. Not merely are the forms of folk-song limited ; its spirit, no matter how pure and natural, excludes much that is indispensable to the creative imagination. Conversely, though the forms of Western poetry are suited to almost every kind of mood, they may lead a poet to concentrate too much on his technique and in the last resort to set his belief in art before his belief in life. In the greatest Russian poets, in Pushkin or Lermontov or Blok, the elements are harmoniously united, and the indigenous spirit purifies and strengthens the wealth of artistic impulses which Russia shares with the West or has adopted from it.

With the Revolution of 1917 many new forces were released in Russia and in Russian poetry, and though at first the poets, eager to be in the vanguard of their art, tried bold experiments and highly modernistic effects, it soon became clear to them that something else was required of them and that they must write not for a few cultivated people who shared their ideas but for a whole nation eager to educate itself. The new situation created a new balance between the indigenous and the Western elements in their art. Boris Pasternak, the finest poet of the age, combines an extremely Russian outlook derived from an intimate understanding of the Russian land and the Russian people with a manner which, in its effective conciseness and vivid imagery, may well be compared with the best work produced in other European countries at the same time. His poetry reflects the first years after the Revolution, when men's minds and senses worked with a new and vivid awareness of what was happening in the world.

INTRODUCTION

In more recent years the increase of discipline and the need for organisation have created a quieter kind of poetry in which the folk-song seems again to play a predominant part. For the moment the West has receded again into the distance, and the poets look to their own country and its traditional art for models and inspiration. But Russia has never kept herself entirely to herself, and we may be confident that in due course she will again look to the West, absorb such lessons as it has to teach, and create that harmony of Russian and Western elements which is the heritage of Pushkin and a most notable characteristic of the Russian genius.

MIKHAIL LOMONOSOV
(1711–1765)

The Lord and Judge

THE God of gods stood up, stood up to try
The assembled gods of earth.   " How long," he said,
" How long will ye protect impiety,
And let the vile one raise his daring head ?

" 'Tis yours my laws to justify, redress
All wrong, however high the wronger be ;
Nor leave the widow and the fatherless
To the cold world's uncertain sympathy.

" 'Tis yours to guard the steps of innocence,
To shield the naked head of misery ;
Be 'gainst the strong the helpless one's defence,
And the poor prisoner from his chains to free."

They hear not, see not, know not, for their eyes
Are covered with thick mists — they *will* not see :
The sick earth groans with man's iniquities,
And heaven is tired with man's perversity.

Gods of the earth ! ye Kings ! who answer not
To man for your misdeeds, and vainly think
There's none to judge you : — know, like ours, your lot
Is pain and death.   Ye stand on judgment's brink.

And ye like fading autumn-leaves will fall ;
Your throne but dust, your empire but a grave,
Your martial pomp a black funereal pall,
Your palace trampled by your meanest slave.

God of the righteous !   O our God ! arise,
O hear the prayer thy lowly servants bring :
Judge, punish, scatter, Lord, thy enemies,
And be alone earth's universal king.

(SIR JOHN BOWRING)

IPPOLIT BOGDANOVICH
(1742–1803)

Old Russian Song

WHAT to the maiden has happened ?
What to the gem of the village ?
  Ah ! to the gem of the village.

Seated alone in her cottage,
Tremblingly turned to the window ;
  Ah ! ever turned to the window.

Like the sweet bird in its prison,
Pining and panting for freedom ;
  Ah ! how it is pining for freedom !

Crowds of her youthful companions
Come to console the lov'd maiden ;
  Ah ! to console the lov'd maiden.

" Smile then, our sister, be joyful,
Clouds of dust cover the valley ;
  O ! see they cover the valley.

" Smile then, our sister ! be joyful,
List to the hoof-beat of horses ;
  O ! to the hoof-beat of horses."

Then the maid looked through the window,
Saw the dust-clouds in the valley ;
  O ! the dust-clouds in the valley.

Heard the hoof-beat of the horses,
Hurried away from the cottage ;
  O ! to the valley she hurries.

" Welcome ! O welcome ! thou loved one " :
See, she has sunk on his bosom ;
  O ! she has sunk on his bosom.

2

Now all her grief is departed ;
She has forsaken the window ;
   O ! quite forsaken the window.

Now her eyes look on her loved one,
Beaming with brightness and beauty ;
   O ! 'tis all brightness and beauty.

(SIR JOHN BOWRING)

ALEXANDER RADISHCHEV
(1749–1802)

Sapphic Stanzas

Icy cold the night was, in heaven the brilliant
Stars were shining, silently flowed the waters,
Gently blew the night-wind, and gently whispered
    Leaves of white poplars.

Vows of deathless constancy thou didst utter;
Sweet the pledge the goddess of darkness gave me;
Roared the blasts of winter, but once and all those
    Vows were forgotten.

Why those rash vows ? O it was surely better
Far if thou hadst always been cruel, less would
I have suffered. Thou with thy false words lured me
    Down to destruction.

Cruel art thou, destiny ; take my life but
Only keep her constancy still unspotted.
Happy mayst thou be if thou canst be only
    Happy without love.

(V. DE S. PINTO)

VASILI KAPNIST
(1757–1823)

On Julia's Death

THE evening darkness shrouds
   The slumbering world in peace,
And from her throne of clouds
   The moon shines through the trees.
My thoughts in silence blend,
   But gather'd all to thee :
Thou moon ! the mourner's friend,
   O come ! and mourn with me.

Upon her grave I bow,
   The green grave where she lies :
O hear my sorrows now,
   And consecrate my sighs !
This is her ashes' bed,
   Here her cold relics sleep,
Where I my tears shall shed
   While this torn heart can weep.

O Julia ! never rose
   Had half the charms of thee,
My comfort, my repose,
   O ! thou wert all to me.
But thou art gone, and I
   Must bear life's load of clay,
And pray, and long to die,
   Though dying day by day.

But I must cease to sing,
   My lyre all mute appears.
Alas ! its plaintive string
   Is wetted with my tears.
O ! misery's song must end.
   My thoughts all fly to thee.
Thou moon ! the mourner's friend,
   O come and mourn with me !

(SIR JOHN BOWRING)

NIKOLAI KARAMZIN
(1766–1826)

Autumn

THE dry leaves are falling ;
The cold breeze above
Has stript of its glories
The sorrowing grove.

The hills are all weeping,
The field is a waste,
The songs of the forest
Are silent and past :

And the songsters are vanished ;
In armies they fly,
To a clime more benignant,
A friendlier sky.

The thick mists are veiling
The valley in white :
With the smoke of the village
They blend in their flight.

And lo ! on the mountain
The wanderer stands,
And sees the pale autumn
Pervading the lands.

Thou sorrowful wanderer,
Sigh not nor weep !
For Nature, though shrouded,
Will wake from her sleep.

The spring, proudly smiling,
Shall all things revive ;
The gay bridal-garments
Of splendour shall give.

But man's chilling winter
Is darksome and dim ;
For no second spring-tide
E'er dawns upon him.

The gloom of his evening
Time dissipates never :
His sun when departed
Is vanisht for ever.

(Sir John Bowring)

WHERE art thou lingering, tell me, thou fair one ?
There where the nightingale wakes her soft music,
   In the night's darkness complaining
   From the top boughs of the myrtle ?

There, where in solitude murmurs the streamlet,
Gliding along its green borders unnoticed,
   Soothing man's turbulent bosom
   Gently to peace and to silence ?

There, where the rose in its pride and its glory
Blushes, bedew'd with the tears of the morning,
   While with the breezes disporting,
   Whispering its thoughts to the zephyrs ?

There, where the sun first illumines the mountain,
Heights inaccessible, cloud-fashion'd palace,
   Where, in the ages departed,
   Spirits and gods had their dwellings ?

Oft have I heard thy sweet voice gently speaking,
Oft on thy throne of bright clouds have I seen thee,
   Stretch'd out my arms to embrace thee —
   Ah ! I had seized but a shadow.

(Sir John Bowring)

7

ALEXEI MERZLYAKOV
(1778–1828)

Song

AMONG the level valley lands,
Upon a gentle height,
A lofty oak-tree buds and grows,
A gay and sturdy sight.

Alone, in all men's sight, the oak
With its great boughs has grown ;
Like a recruit on guard it is,
Poor soul, alone, alone.

If the resplendent sun comes out,
Who gives the oak-tree shade ?
And if the rain deals blows at it,
Who comes to bring it aid ?

Nor little curling pine-trees grow
Nor willow-trees around,
Nor bushes in their greenery
About its trunk abound.

'Tis sorrowful to grow alone
Thus even for a tree,
And sad, oh sad for a young man
Without a love to be.

His stores of silver and of gold
With whom can he divide ?
He has much fame and name, but whom
Has he to share his pride ?

(C. M. Bowra)

VASILI ZHUKOVSKY
(1783–1852)

To Her

THERE is no name for thee!
'Tis beyond all mortal cunning
To reveal what charm is thine.

There is no lyre for thee!
What can song do? 'Tis false witness
Come too late with news of thee.

If we could only hear
What the heart says, what a power
Would be in its hymn to thee!

All the charm of thy life,
With thy image pure and holy,
Is a secret in my heart.

Love is all I can do.
But the love that thou hast borne me
Only endless time can tell!

(C. M. BOWRA)

The Sea

SEA, with waters unspeaking, with waters of azure,
I linger enchanted above your abyss.
You live, and you breathe, and you know love's confusion;
You are brim-full with thoughts that disquiet and fret.
Sea, with waters unspeaking, with waters of azure,
Uncover the secret you hide in your depths.
What is it that moves in your limitless bosom?
What is it that breathes in the toils of your breast?
Can it be that the sky, far away and resplendent,
Draws you up to itself from the bondage of earth?
You, brimming with life and with secrets and sweetness,
In that virginal presence are virginal too.

9

You delight in the bright azure light of its sunrise,
You burn with its flames in the evening and morn.
You sport with its gold-gleaming clouds for your playmates,
And joyfully flash with the fire of its stars.
When the black swelling clouds come together above you
To carry the glitter of heaven away,
You fight, and you swell, and you lift up your breakers,
You tear and you torture the enemy mist.
When the dark disappears and the clouds have departed,
Still full of the troubles that lately have past,
For long you still throw up your breakers astounded ;
And when the sweet face of the sky shows again,
It does not at once restore quiet within you.
Though you seem to be still, you are full of deceit.
In the peace of your depths you conceal your confusion,
And you quake with desire for the sky that you love.

(C. M. Bowra)

You were before me,
Standing in silence ;
Your face was downcast
And deep in thought.
It made me think of
The past we loved so.
That was the last time
It saw this world here.

Away you vanished,
A silent angel.
To-day your grave is
Quiet as heaven.
There all things earthly
Are memories only.
There all things earthly
Are thoughts of heaven.

Stars of the sky,
Silence of night !

(C. M. Bowra)

PETER VYAZEMSKY
(1792–1878)

THOU art my bright star in a world half-hidden,
And there from earth's confusion I arise;
There waits the lyre that thou has strung unbidden,
There visions warm with thee await my eyes.

Thou art the cloud that on my daytime hovers,
When of thee all my dreams and fancies are,
Or when my thought our destined road discovers,
And from thy fate my fate is severed far.

Thou art soft dusk that cools my spirit's fretting,
When in the sunset of the careworn day
My mind reposes and my heart is setting
And shades of death descend upon my way.

(C. M. BOWRA)

WHEN youth still made my spirit bold,
Gay songs of the first snow were mine;
In frosts that first of Winter told
Of joys to come I saw the sign.

In those hot years 'twas my delight
On Winter's silver crown to glance,
To mark the smile serene and bright
On Winter's shining countenance.

Now old with years and knowledge grown,
With secret agony and dread
I look where the white flakes are blown
Over the earth dispirited.

In images of life's decay
I see a fatal warning then, —
If days and seasons pass away,
So passes too the race of men.

(C. M. BOWRA)

KONDRATI RYLEEV
(1795-1826)

Elegy

AN end has come to all my yearning,
My early dreams have all come true.
My passion and its cruel burning
And all my love were known to you.

In vain I fretted. In full measure
For my desires comes recompense.
I live again for the heart's pleasure ;
Grief, like a dream, has vanished hence.

So sprinkled with the kindly showers
Of evening when the west is bright,
Half-dead and cold the meadow flowers
Arise and bloom again at night.

(C. M. BOWRA)

ANTON DELVIEG
(1798–1831)

Romance

Oh lovely day, oh happy day !
  Oh love and the sun's light !
From bare fields shadows float away ;
  The heart again is bright.
Let woods and meadows wakened be,
  Let all things burst with spring.
" She comes to me, she comes to me ",
  My heart is whispering.

Why, swallow, beat upon the pane ?
  What, free one, would you say ?
Is it that spring is here again
  And love is on its way ?
I need you not and let you be.
  Love burns in me to sing :
" She comes to me, she comes to me ",
  My heart is whispering.

(C. M. Bowra)

Russian Song

Ah, you night, you
  Little night !
Ah, you night, you
  Stormy night !
Wherefore show you
  From the dusk
To the full hour
  Of midnight
No light shining
  From the stars,
No light gleaming
  From the moon,
But you darken
  All with clouds ?

'Tis with you, then,
  Little night,
As with me here
  In my youth.
Wicked sorrow
  Summons us !
When the villain
  Settles down
In deep places
  Of the heart,
You forget all
  Pretty girls
And the bowing
  And the smiles.
You forget then
  From the dusk
To the full hour
  Of midnight
All the singing
  And delight
In the chorus
  And the dance !
No, you burst forth
  Into tears ;
And, a homeless,
  Sad young man,
Throw yourself down
  On a bed
Hard and squalid
  As the grave.

(C. M. Bowra)

Russian Song

Sang a little bird, and sang,
  Then was silent ;
Knew the heart of happiness,
  Then forgot it.

ANTON DELVIEG

Why, O little singing bird,
    Wert thou silent?
How wert thou acquainted, heart
    With black sorrow?

Ah, the little bird was killed
    By fierce snow-storms;
And the young man perished too
    From fierce gossip.

Had the bird but flown away
    To blue waters!
Had the young man run away
    To the forest!

On the sea are roaring waves,
    And not snow-storms;
In the woods are untamed beasts,
    And not people!

                    (C. M. Bowra)

ALEXANDER PUSHKIN
(1799–1837)

To a Brownie

To thee, our peaceful ground invisibly defending,
  Here is my prayer, O Brownie kind and good : —
  Keep safe my hamlet, and my garden wild, and wood,
And all my cloistered household unpretending !

May never rainstorm hurt these fields with perilous cold ;
  May no belated autumn hurricane assail them !
  But helpful, timely snowfall veil them
Above the moist, manuring mould !

By these ancestral shades stay secret sentinel ;
  See thou intimidate the midnight robber spying ;
  Guard from all ill unfriendly eyeing
The happy cottage where we dwell !

Patrol it watchfully about ; thy love betoken
  To my small plot, and stream embankt that drowsy flows,
  And this sequestered kitchen-close
With ancient crumbling wicket-gate and fences broken !

— Love, too, the hillock's slope of green
  And meadows that I tread in idle rumination,
  The cool lime-shades, the maples' murmuring screen : —
These are the haunts of inspiration.

(O. Elton)

The Coach of Time

OFTEN with heavy burdens freighted,
The coach rolls on with easy pace.
The driver on the box is seated,
Grey Time, who never leaves his place.

We take our seats at early morning,
And by the coachman start the trip ;

Our indolence and comfort scorning,
We cry : " Now let the horses rip ! "

When noon comes, we have lost our daring.
We're shaken up ; we fear and doubt,
And down steep slopes and gullies faring
We cry : " Go slow, you fool ! Look out ! "

The coach rolls as before unshaken.
We're used to it ere day is done.
At last, by slumber overtaken,
We reach the inn, — but Time drives on.

(C. M. BOWRA)

A Prologue

A CHAIN hangs down with golden fetters
From a green oak-tree, in a bay,
And on that chain a cat of letters
Walks round for ever, night and day ;
Goes singing, as she rightward ambles ;
Turns leftward, and a tale relates.
Strange things are there ; the wood-sprite rambles ;
The water-maid in branches waits ;
And there, on paths unnoted, thickens
The slot of beasts to man unknown ;
A cottage there, on legs of chickens,
Unwindowed, doorless, stands alone.
With visions wood and vale are teeming ;
And there at dawn, the tide comes streaming
On a deserted sandy verge,
And thirty chosen champions splendid,
By their sea-uncle still attended,
In turn from the bright wave emerge.
A prince is travelling by, and sweeping
Before them all a warrior brave
Away across the wood and wave ;
There, served by a brown wolf and loyal,
In prison stands a lady royal.
Beside the Dame Yagà there stalks
A pestle : as on feet, it walks,

Sick king Kashchèy on gold is gloating ;
There, the true Russian scent is floating !
— And there was I, and drank my mead,
And saw the leafy oak, and sat there
Down by the sea. The learned cat there
Told me her tales ; and one, indeed,
Comes back to mind ; I now disclose it,
And care not if the whole world knows it.

(O. ELTON)

The Prisoner

SITTING here behind bars in a dank cell am I.
A young eagle outside, who was born free to fly,
My sorrowful friend, flaps his wings in the day
By the window and pecks at his blood-dripping prey.

Then he ceases from pecking and through the bars stares,
As though he partook of my thoughts and my cares ;
In his looks and his cries he has something to say,
As though he would call : " Let us now fly away !

' We are free birds together. 'Tis time, brother, now !
Out there past the clouds on the white mountain's brow,
Out there where the country is blue by the sea,
Out there where the wind walks alone — and with me ! "

(C. M. BOWRA)

Gipsy's Song

GREY old man, savage man,
Slice me up, burn me dead.
I am proud. Not the knife,
Not the fire shall I dread.

Naught for you but disdain,
Naught but loathing, have I ;
For I love someone else,
And for love I shall die.

18

Slice me up, burn me dead.
Nothing shall I betray.
Grey old man, savage man,
Who he is I'll not say !

Summer burns not so hot,
Not so bright spring as he.
He is young, he is brave.
What a love his for me !

How I gave him my love
In the still hours of night !
How we laughed, both of us,
At your hair turning white !

(C. M. BOWRA)

WHAT though life conspire to cheat you,
Do not sorrow or complain.
Lie still on the day of pain,
And the day of joy will greet you.

Hearts live in the coming day.
There's an end to passing sorrow.
Suddenly all flies away,
And delight returns to-morrow.

(C. M. BOWRA)

Winter Road

THROUGH the eddying haze and shadows
  Now the moon is making way,
And on melancholy meadows
  Pours a melancholy ray.

Down the wintry road and dreary
  Flies the troika, swift, alone,
And for ever tinks its weary
  Tiny bell, in monotone ;

And the driver's ditty drawling
　Has a homelike sound for me,
Sickness of the heart recalling,
　Or old reckless revelry.

Ah, these snows and wastes, no lonely
　Fire, or blackened hut, beguiles !
But, in slow procession, only
　Motley posts that mark the miles !

— Nina, I return to-morrow,
　And beside thy hearth, dear friend,
Drown my tedium and sorrow,
　Gazing, gazing without end.

While the clock, with ticking finger,
　Circles round so evenly,
None shall pester us, none linger !
　Midnight parts not thee and me.

— Nina, sad my way and weary ;
　Mute, the driver nods at last ;
Still the small bell tinkles, dreary,
　And the moon is overcast.

(O. Elton)

The Avalanche

Beaten by jagged rocks to steam,
Before me pours the boiling stream ;
Above my head the eagles scream,
　The pine-wood speaks,
And through the mist there faintly gleam
　The mountain-peaks.

From where the snow-clad summits soar
An avalanche in days of yore
Thundering down with mighty roar
　The channel filled
Through which the river Terek tore
　Impetuous-willed.

20

Its waters lake-wise spread about,
A moment Terek stilled its shout,
Until the last waves' raging rout
    Burst through the snow
And, filled with fury, battered out
    A path below.

And there the snow for many a day
In huge, unmelting masses lay ;
Beneath, fierce Terek bored a way
    That naught could halt
And spattered with a noisy spray
    The icy vault.

And o'er the snow a wide road led :
There oxen plodded, horses sped,
Leading his camel by the head
    The merchant passed,
Where rushes now through caverns dread
    The wind's chill blast.

(W. A. MORISON)

Monastery on Kasbek

THY peak transcends thy brother heights,
Kasbek ; with everlasting lights
Thy tented dome in splendour flowers ;
Beyond the clouds thine Abbey towers,
As though in Heaven were poised a shrine,
And o'er the mountains dimly lowers.

Far lies the shore for which I pine !
Farewell, ye valleys !   Thither let me
Aloft to surging summits ride,
In little cell, past clouds, to set me,
And near to God O let me hide !

(SIR CECIL KISCH)

The Caucasus

BELOW me the Caucasus.   Lone on the height
I stand on the brink of the snow and look over.
Far distant an eagle has risen to hover
And linger unmoved on a line with my sight.
From here I can see the first birth of the rivers
And where the first stir of the avalanche quivers.

Below me submissively clouds come and go,
Through which a precipitous waterfall passes.
Beneath them are boulders in great naked masses ;
Then, lower, lank mosses and small bushes grow.
Then woodlands begin, and green shadows are creeping,
And birds are a-whisper, and young deer are leaping.

Next, men on the hillside their eyries have made,
And sheep in their herds on the sloping grass wander,
And shepherds go forth to the glad valleys yonder,
Where whirls the Aragva by banks in the shade,
And tribesmen are lurking in gullies for plunder,
And fiercely delighted the Terek plays under.

It plays like a young beast of prey, and it roars
For food from the prison of iron which holds it,
And uselessly fights with the gorge that enfolds it,
And licks with its arrogant water the shores. . . .
In vain.   For all solace, all sustenance fail it ;
The imprisoning rocks harshly, silently jail it.

(C. M. BOWRA)

Song in Time of Plague

WHEN winter full of lusty might
Comes, a bold chieftain to the fight,
Around him shaggy hosts assemble,
The frosts and snows like ravening beasts ;
Before their coming hearthstones tremble
And men rejoice in yuletide feasts.

Then mighty Plague, the stormy queen,
Approaching us herself is seen,

With greedy tongue her rich feast lapping;
And at our windows night and day
With graveyard spades we hear her rapping . . .
What help can then avail us, say ?

We warded off the winter fell,
From Plague we'll comfort take as well,
Light fires, with goblets our thirst slaking,
Our senses drown in revelry,
Gay dances and rich banquets making,
Sing praise, O great queen Plague, to thee.

In battle there's a kind of bliss,
In terror of a black abyss,
And in a wild and stormy ocean,
'Twixt waves and skies as dark as death,
Arabian sandstorm's fierce commotion,
And mighty Plague, in thy hot breath.

All things that rage, all that destroy
Bring an unspeakable strange joy,
To mortal hearts a premonition,
It may be, of immortal life ;
Happy the man who sees that vision
Clearly amid the passions' strife.

So thee, great Plague, we praise and cheer,
Shades of the tomb we do not fear,
Nor can thy haughty summons fright us ;
We'll quaff from goblets foaming free,
Rose-maidens' kisses shall delight us,
Though filled, perchance, O Plague, with thee !

(V. DE S. PINTO)

Echo

To beast's cry in its forest lair,
To thunderclap or trumpet's blare,
To girl's song in the hills somewhere,
To every sound

23

Your answer in the empty air
   Rolls quickly round.

To thunder rumbling in the skies,
To voice of storm when billows rise,
And to the village shepherds' cries
   You listen too. . . .
But for you there are no replies. . . .
   Poet, that's you !

                    (C. M. BOWRA)

WHEN the last great and solemn act was played
And God in torment on the cross was laid,
Then at the foot of the life-giving rood
Mary the sinner and Mary the Virgin stood,
Two women side by side,
Drowned in their grief's immeasurable tide.

But here beneath the cross we contemplate,
As though on duty at the Governor's gate,
Instead of those two holy women, lo,
Two sentries grim, with musket and shako.
Now tell me, Why ?   This crucifix, maybe,
You guard in state as Government property ?
Or thieves, or mice, you fancy, might lay siege ?
Or to the King of Kings you'ld add prestige ?
Or do you hope by patronage to save
The Lord who is crowned with thorns, the Lord
   who gave
In willingness His mortal flesh to bear
The Roman torturer's lash, the nails, the spear ?
Or else you fear the mob may bring disgrace
On Him who dying saved all Adam's race ?
Or, lest his presence irk the modish crowd,
The common man, perhaps, is Not Allowed ?

                (FRANCES CORNFORD)

EVGENI BARATYNSKY
(1800–1844)

Complaint

It comes, it comes, the day of meeting,
When I, my friend, shall look on thee.
But why no rapturous hope of greeting?
Why trembles not my heart in me?
It makes no plaint, but sorrow's day
Too late perhaps has passed away.
I look on joy with anxious dread.
Its splendour leaves my heart unshaken,
And unavailingly I waken
Hope in my soul dispirited.
Though playful fortune smile and greet me,
My joy is not complete in her.
Some false delight still seems to cheat me;
No transports do her glances stir.

(C. M. BOWRA)

Dissuasion

Tempt me not now; it is not wanted.
Show me no more your gentle ways.
But know that I am disenchanted
And shun the lure of former days.

I trust no promises from you,
My trust in love itself now falters.
The vision that I cherished alters;
I shall not yield to it anew.

With pleasant words of what has gone
Do not increase my blind devotion.
Tend not with care my sick emotion,
But let it slumber gently on.

I sleep, and sweet is sleep, forgetting
The visions that I used to see.
Though tumult in my soul is fretting,
Yet love you will not wake in me.

(C. M. BOWRA)

Bare Days

BARE days ! Our world in its eternal tameness
　　Jogs the unchanging way
We know so well, and naught but weary sameness
　　Waits on each dawning day.
Not vainly didst thou pant and struggle, striving
　　To thy predestined goal,
At plenitude before the flesh arriving,
　　Crazily plunging soul !
The narrow network of this world's sensations
　　Has long since closed its mesh ;
Cajoled by thy recurrent dream-creations
　　Thou sleepest, while the flesh
Looks dully on, as needless dawn replaces
　　Night's pointless shadow-play ;
As night the evening's empty brow embraces,
　　Crowning a barren day.

(W. A. MORISON)

ALEXANDER ODOEVSKY
(1802–1839)

Do you know those whom I so loved before,
With whom I shared the darkened years of yore?
Do you know them? Like me, in your embraces
You held them, and you brought the friendly tone
Of voices that my soul long since had known.
Again I heard the speech of my own places ;
I seemed to be upon my native ground
Where friends in harmony had gathered round.

So travellers on pilgrimages going
Through burning heat across a sandy sea
By shady palms and water coolly flowing
Are lured, — 'tis only a sweet fantasy
That cheats them, yet by it is strength begotten,
And on the caravan goes steadfastly
Till in the heat the dusty grave's forgotten.

(C. M. Bowra)

NIKOLAI YAZYKOV
(1803–1846)

Bard's Song

FLY like an arrow, Night, O Night !
Svyatoslav cannot rest or slumber ;
He's thirsty for his fated fight. . . .
Fly like an arrow, Night, O Night !
Svyatoslav cannot rest or slumber !

Tsimiskhy ! is your buckler sound ?
Have you strong armour from the smithy ?
Our prince deals deadly blows around. . . .
Tsimishky ! is your buckler sound ?
Is not fine armour in the smithy ?

Give us the fastest steeds to ride,
And let them not be overtaken ;
From swords let them not turn aside. . . .
Give us the fastest steeds to ride,
And let them not be overtaken !

Unnumbered is the host you bring ;
Not many we, but we are Russians.
Our stroke is sure and shattering. . . .
Unnumbered is the host you bring ;
Not many we, but we are Russians !

Fly like an arrow, Night, O Night !
Fields, open up the way to triumph,
Awake, O horror of the fight !
Fly, like an arrow, Night, O Night !
Fields, open up the way to triumph !

(C. M. BOWRA)

WHO sings not when the wine-cups throng
Knows not delight in fullest measure.
The vineyard's god must share the pleasure
Of young days with the god of song.

The words are holy : " Drink and sing ".
No gay carousal can deride them.
When wine-cups keep a harp beside them,
Two gods a twofold banquet bring.

The nights in loveliness excel,
When radiant the moonbeams glimmer ;
And, where bewitching dresses shimmer,
Enchanting beauty casts her spell.

Who sings not when the wine-cups throng
Knows not delight in fullest measure.
The vineyard's god must share the pleasure
Of young days with the god of song.

(C. M. Bowra)

Elegy

Blest, who upon night's bed can lie
And fold you in his arms at rest,
With brow on brow and eye on eye,
With lips on lips and breast on breast,
Who with his sudden burning kisses
Your sweet seductive lisp can break,
And dark breasts, trembling with wild blisses,
Now lull to slumber, now awake.
But more blest he, O child of Night,
Who, when love's waking passions rouse,
Looks in your eyes that flame so bright,
Upon the marvel of your brows,
Upon your fresh lips, red and sweet,
Upon your young and raven tresses,
Forgetful of joy's stormy heat
And all the strength that youth possesses.

(C. M. Bowra)

O Liberty, proud inspiration !
The people knows not what you are.

29

It prays, — divine retaliation !
But rises not against the Tsar.

Beneath the despot's yoke for ever,
In his infernal bonds confined,
The heart no sorrow feels, and never
Can mind believe another mind.

I have seen servile Russia sinking
In churches where the altars blaze.
With head bowed down and fetters clinking
She kneels down for the Tsar and prays.

(C. M. BOWRA)

FEDOR TYUTCHEV
(1803–1873)

Spring Waters

THE fields are white still with the snow,
   But now the streams are loud with spring.
They wake the sleeping banks and flow ;
   They flow, they sparkle, and they sing.

Through all the earth the message stirs :
   " The spring is near, the spring is near.
We are the young spring's messengers ;
   She sent us on, and we are here."

The spring is near, the spring is near ;
   And warm and tranquil days of May
In rosy radiant train appear
   Behind her on their jocund way.

(C. M. BOWRA)

Spring

WINTER is wroth, with reason !
   Her hour is now no more ;
Spring lifts the latch in season
   And drives her from the door.

Now all are up and doing,
   And Winter must away.
The larks, their song renewing,
   Ring changes through the day.

But Winter fusses proudly,
   And rudely scolds the Spring.
Spring mocks at her, and loudly
   Her peals of laughter ring.

The bad witch goes on trying ;
Her anger drives her wild.
She sends a snow-ball flying
To hit the pretty child.

Spring does not care, but washes
Her beauty in the snow,
And ruddier are her blushes
Defiant of her foe.

(C. M. BOWRA)

Autumn Evening

IN the magnificence of autumn eves
A soft, mysterious enchantment lies. . . .
The eerie gleam of motley trees, the leaves
All purple, and their faint and ghostly sighs ;
The azure air, so misty and so dumb,
Above the earth that turns to grey in sorrow,
And, like foreboding of a storm to come,
The gusty wind that speaks a rainy morrow.
Decay, and weariness, and over all
A gentle smile that tells of something waning,
A smile that in our human kind we call
Greatness of heart that suffers uncomplaining.

(C. M. BOWRA)

NIGHT wind, what cry you on your way ?
And what lament, so madly calling ?
What does your voice so strangely say,
Now loud, now pitifully falling ?

In words the heart can comprehend
You speak of pain past comprehending,
And still you suffer, still you send
To me your cries of wrath unending.

Let not those fearful songs begin,
Of ancient, native Chaos singing !
How greedily my world within
Hears the belovéd message ringing !

From mortal heart it longs to leap
And join itself to the Unbounded . . .
Wake not the tempests from their sleep :
For Chaos stirs when you have sounded.

(C. M. Bowra)

I KNEW her erst in days afar
That full of fairy fancies are,
As when at touch of morning hue,
At dawn's first ray a shining star
Sinks swiftly lost in heaven's blue.

And there I saw her form, her face
Instinct with freshness, breathing grace,
— The charm of dusk at break of day,
When, borne unheard, unseen, from space
The morning dews among the flowers' array.

Her life complete, in every side
Perfected, whole, would not abide
An alien world's discordant jar,
And so, I think, she has not died
But only set — as might a star.

(Sir Cecil Kisch)

SHE lay unconscious there through all the day,
And now the evening shadows closed above her ;
Warm summer rain fell softly, and its gay
Plash on the leaves passed lightly over.

Then slowly once again she found her sense,
And paid attention to the rustling shower ;

And long she listened with her thoughts far hence,
Yet conscious was her mind in all its power.

And then, as speaking to herself, she said
In conscious words articulated clearly,
— I watched her living still, though all but dead, —
" Oh, how I loved it all, how dearly ! "

Ah, how you used to love ! To none alive
Has love to equal such as yours been given.
O God ! Can she be dead, while I survive,
And still my heart in fragments not be riven ?

(C. M. Bowra)

THESE poor hamlets, humbly faring,
Nature sunk in desolation,
Land of mine, such sorrows bearing,
Land of all the Russian nation !

Nothing knowing, nothing seeing,
How can haughty foreign faces
Mark what mystery has being
In thy lowly, naked places ?

There was one, my land, who knew thee :
With a cross upon him pressing,
Like a servant passing through thee,
Heaven's King once gave his blessing.

(C. M. Bowra)

DMITRI VENEVITINOV
(1805–1827)

Three Roses

WHERE life's road through the waste is driven,
Tokens of loveliness divine,
Three roses by the gods are given ;
No fairer flowers in Eden shine.

One with the Cashmir sky above it
Blossoms beside a crystal spring.
Most tenderly the West winds love it ;
It stirs the nightingale to sing.
By day and night it stays unfaded ;
If any pluck it from its bed,
From the sharp light of morning shaded
A fresh young rose comes forth instead.

The second is yet more enchanting ;
It blossoms in the morning skies,
And when the crimson dawn comes slanting,
Its dazzling beauty lures the eyes.
A cooling air is hid within it
And blows with greeting glad and gay.
It droops within a single minute
And buds anew with each new day.

The third, with breath yet cooler blowing,
Blossoms not in the skies above.
Upon the cheeks of girlhood glowing,
For hot lips it is nursed by love.
But that rose all too quickly closes ;
It is too gentle and too shy.
In vain the morning seeks its roses ;
No others blossom when they die.

(C. M. BOWRA)

I FEEL that deep within me burns
A holy flame of inspiration,

But for dark goals my spirit yearns. . . .
Who sets the path of my salvation ?
I see my life before me spread
And foaming like a sea unbounded. . . .
Shall I find ledges firmly founded
Where I can walk with certain tread ?
Or, while eternal doubts confound me,
Shall I look forth in sorrowing
Where the inconstant waves surround me,
Not knowing what to love or sing ?

" To all in nature turn your vision,"
A secret voice replied to me,
" But give her choice and free decision.
Your fated time is yet to be.
Now seek the miracles of living,
Fill every moment all life long,
To all the music of her giving
Give answer with responsive song.
When the astonished minutes flying
Go past you like a misty dream,
When secrets of the world undying
Clearer to quiet glances seem,
Then stilled is your proud aspiration
To grasp at once the universe,
And sounds that your soft strings rehearse
Blend in the music of creation."

True was the voice's exhortation.
And ever since my loyal strings
Have to my soul kept faith unchanging.
My song through joy, through sorrow ranging,
Now passion's flame, now love's heat sings,
And with thoughts fugitively straying
My fiery verses will not fail.
So in the wood the nightingale
At dusk, her brief delight obeying,
When shadows turn the valley grey,
Gives praises to the evening sadly,
But greets the red of morning gladly
And sings a welcome to the day.

(C. M. Bowra)

VLADIMIR BENEDIKTOV
(1807–1873)

Cold Confession

No, no ! It is not that which fills my eyes !
In me you see no frenzied passion gleam.
And what is love but crafty enterprise
Plotted by fiery blood and sightless dream ?

I have paid out my tribute of defeat ;
I have outlived my days of youthful fire.
You saw my soul burn in its whitest heat
In front of you, O star of my desire.

You saw it. . . . Now another destiny
I greet, another life is mine from hence ;
And when I look on you, I feel in me
Coldness and sanctity and reverence.

Snow on my heart, but not the valley's snow,
Which footsteps trample and the mist weighs down, —
No, snow on mountain-tops where white clouds go,
Snow on the dead volcano's icy crown.

Its face to you, as to the sun, it turns ;
It greets you when the earth is lost in shade.
With all the fires within your soul it burns,
And of your fiery soul is not afraid.

(C. M. Bowra)

KAROLINA PAVLOVA
(1807–1893)

WHILE in dark and deadly places
Of the wilderness you stray,
Of what vision seek you traces,
Weary pilgrim, on your way ?

Quite forgotten, none to greet you,
In the starless Polar night,
While you gaze, the dawn will cheat you
Waiting till the day turn white.

Vainly such a daybreak blazing
Does your trembling heart divine ;
Dawn will vanish from your gazing,
And that sun will never shine.

(C. M. BOWRA)

ALEXEY KOLTSOV
(1808–1842)

Harvest

RED and fiery
The dawn lights the sky ;
On earth's countenance
Lies the mist outspread.

The day catches fire
From the hot sunbeams ;
And the fog aloft
On the upland fields

Now is thickening
To a black rain-cloud . . .
And the black rain-cloud
Overcasts the sky,

Overcasts the sky,
And is deep in thought
As remembering
Its own motherland.

Wild winds boisterous
Soon will carry it
Into each quarter
Of the shining earth.

It arrays itself
With the storm-wind, thunder,
And the lightning flame
And the arched rainbow.

It arrays itself ;
It has swollen up ;
It has struck about
And has spilled itself

In abundant tears,
In the rain that floods
Over earth's bosom,
Over wide acres.

And from heaven's hill
Now the sun looks out.
Earth has drunk water
And is well content.

Over gardens, fields,
Over green places,
All the country folk
Gaze without ceasing.

All the country folk
Long have been waiting
For God's great goodness
And have feared and prayed.

With the spring's coming
Blest, inviolate
Thoughts of peacefulness
In their hearts awake.

And their first thoughts are
To collect the grain
For the bins in sacks
And to pile the loads.

After that they turn
To a second thought,
To ride out betimes
From their villages.

And their third thought is —
Deeply they think it —
To bow down and pray
To the Lord our God.

When the dawn comes, all
Have gone through the fields,

And friend after friend
Makes his way out there,

And from brimming hands
Scatters forth the grain ;
They go forth with ploughs
To break up the earth,

Yes, with curved ploughshares
To divide the soil,
With the toothed harrow
To throw up the clods.

I shall go to see
And shall love the sight
That the Lord has sent
For the people's toil.

Now the rye is weighed
To the waist with grain,
And its dreaming ears
Nearly touch the ground.

Like a guest of God,
Upon every side
It invites with smiles
To the gay daylight.

The breeze over it,
Bright and quivering,
Hurries here and there
In its golden waves.

Folk by their households
Have begun reaping,
And cut at the roots
Of the tall rye-stalks.

In the rows of ricks
All the sheaves are piled ;
From the waggons creaks
Music all night long.

On the threshing-floors
The stacks, like princes,
Are enthroned on high
With uplifted heads.

The sun sees it all,
That the reaping's done;
Then it grows cooler
And to autumn moves.

But the bright candle
Of the villager
Burns before the shrine
Of God's blest Mother.

(C. M. Bowra)

The Young Reaper

Lofty stands the sun
In the sky above;
And its fiery heat
Bakes up Mother Earth.

And it stifles her,
Mournful on the field.
She has no delight
In the new-mown rye.

She is all on fire
From the burning field,
And the flaming sun
Scorches her white face.

Drooping falls her head
Down upon her breast,
And the rye falls down
From her weary hand.

She, with thoughts astray,
Reaps and does not reap,
And she looks around
In forgetfulness.

Oh, her aching heart
Gives her misery.
There is something wrong,
Something not yet known.

Yesterday she went,
On a day of rest,
Through the wood she went
To the hazel grove.

There a fine young man
Came upon her way;
Not the first time they
Met each other thus.

So he met her there,
As it were by chance.
And he stood and looked
In a kind of grief.

Then he sighed and sang
An unhappy song,
And the song rang loud
Through the distant woods.

Deep within the soul
Of the lovely girl
It resounded too,
And it stopped in her.

The heat stifles her
Mournful on the field.
She can find no joy
In the new-mown rye.

(C. M. Bowra)

Song

Where, my days, are you,
Days of my springtide,
Nights of summertime,
Happy, halcyon?

Where, my life, art thou ?
Where the joy I loved ?
Where the scarlet dawn
Of my flaming youth ?

Ah, how proud my gaze
In the days of old,
Ah, how brave before
Misty days to come !

In them shone for me
Gleam of deep-blue eyes ;
In them was no end
To the dreams I had.

But in midmost spring,
In my budding youth,
I have ruined all,
Life so crystalline.

And without thee now
In despair I watch
How the gloom of night
Comes to close the day.

(C. M. Bowra)

Song

Oh, my love was more hot
Than the day or the flame.
To no other such love
Ever came, ever came.

One life in the world
I led with him alone,
Gave my soul to his soul,
Joined my life to his own.

What a night, what a moon,
As I wait for him here !

I am pale, I am cold,
And I shiver with fear.

He is coming.   He sings :
" Where, my darling, are you ? "
See, he takes up my hand,
See, he kisses me, too.

" Oh, my darling, put out
Your hot kisses like flame !
For without them my blood
Is on fire since you came.

" Without them, since you came,
My face burns and is red,
And my breast wildly beats,
And my eyes glitter bright
Like a star in the night."

(C. M. Bowra)

MIKHAIL LERMONTOV
(1814–1841)

Borodino

" COME tell me, was it all for naught
That Moscow burned, although we fought
 And would not yield ?
Come, Uncle, tell the tale again
Of how we fought with might and main,
And men remember, not in vain,
 Our Borodino's field."

" Yes, in our time the men were men,
And from the heat of battle then
 How few returned,
How few returned their fields to till !
Heroes — not lads like you — they still
Fought on, but could not stay God's will,
 That Moscow burned.

" We beat retreat by day and night,
We fumed and waited for the fight ;
 The old men jeered :
' We'd better winter in the bogs,
And build up huts and bring in logs,
But never turn to face the Frogs,
 And singe their beard.'

" But then a noble stretch of ground
To build a great redoubt we found,
 And there entrench.
All night we listened. Naught astir !
But when the dawn touched fir by fir
And lit the guns — why then, good sir,
 We saw the French.

" I had my powder tightly rammed.
I'll serve you now, and you be damned,
 My fine Mounseer !

No hope for you to lurk and crawl ;
We'll stand against you like a wall ;
And if needs must, we'll give our all
  For Moscow, here.

" For three whole days without a change
We only shot at distant range ;
  No use at all !
You heard men saying left and right,
It's time to buckle to and fight —
Until across the fields the night
  Began to fall.

" I lay to sleep beside my gun,
But heard the cheer, till night was done,
  The Frenchmen made.
Our men were quiet. One would sit
And mend his coat where it was slit,
Or bite his long moustache and spit
  And clean his blade.

" The very hour night was fled
Our guns began to move ahead :
  My God, the rattle !
Our officers were gallant then ;
They served their Tsar and loved their men,
They lie asleep in field or fen,
  Who led the battle.

" The Colonel set our hearts astir :
' Moscow's behind. My lads, for her,
  As all have heard,
Our fathers fought with might and main.
Let's swear to die for her again.'
And there on Borodino's plain
  We kept our word.

" That was a day. Towards our redoubt
We saw the Frenchmen gallop out
  Through smoky air,

Dragoons as bright as on parade,
And blue hussars with golden braid,
And Uhlans — what a show they made !
    They all were there.

" That was a day will never die :
The flags like spirits streaming by —
    A fire ahead —
The clash of steel — the cannon's blast —
Our arms too weak to slay at last :
But few the bullets were that passed
    Our wall of dead.

" That day the foeman learned aright
The way we Russian soldiers fight —
    Fierce hand to hand,
Horses and men together laid,
And still the thundering cannonade ;
Our breasts were trembling, as it made
    Tremble the land.

" Then darkness fell on hill and plain ;
Yet we were game to fight again
    When dawn was red,
Till all at once the drums began,
And as they rolled the Frenchmen ran ;
And we must reckon, man by man,
    Our friends, the dead.

" Yes, in our time the men were men ;
Soldiers — not lads like you — were then
    Heroes indeed !
Hard was the fate their courage earned ;
Not many from the field returned,
And never had our Moscow burned —
    But God decreed."

(FRANCES M. CORNFORD)

AFANASI FET
(1820–1892)

I HAVE come again with greeting
To say that the morn shines brightly,
And the heat of sun is beating
And stirring the young leaves lightly :

To tell you of woodland stirring,
Of the brakes and branches waking ;
Ev'ry bird its wings is whirring,
And its thirst for spring is slaking :

To tell you that my old passion
Brings me back to love you duly,
That my soul in its old fashion
Still delights to serve you truly :

To tell you how all is ringing
Above me in air delighted ;
I know not what to be singing,
But to you my song is plighted.

(C. M. BOWRA)

THE last clouds in a throng above us sailing
      Flee from night's gathering shade ;
Transparent fragments drop down, softly trailing
      On the moon's sickle blade.

Now Spring reigns in her secret strength and glory ;
      Her brow with stars is crowned.
Of joy, my gentle love, you tell a story,
      Joy in this vain world found.

But where is joy ? Not in these squalid places :
      Like smoke in yonder sky
It drifts : following its faint and airy traces
      For ever we must fly.

(V. DE S. PINTO)

Expect to-morrow to be fair ;
    The martins flash, and raise their pipe ;
The lucid west is lighted there
    With one candescent purple stripe.

The boats are drowsing on the bay ;
    The pennant, scarcely fluttering, lies ;
The sea recedes, and far away
    Melts in the far receding skies.

So timidly the shades come on,
    So stealthily retires the light,
You cannot say the day is gone,
    You do not say that there is night.

(O. Elton)

When she her crimson lips uncloses
    To frosty breath of morning grey,
How strange the smile of yonder rose is,
    This transient September day !

How bravely, whilst the titmouse flutters
    Among the bushes fallen bare,
The spring's old greeting still she utters,
    Stands forth with that imperial air,

And blossoms, — with the hope unshaken
    To quit her chilly bed, and rest
In ecstasy, the last rose taken
    By the young Mistress to her breast !

(O. Elton)

Skies again are deep and bare ;
Scents of spring are on the air ;
Nearer, nearer every hour
Draws the bridegroom in his power.

Coffined in her icy shell,
Under some dream-woven spell,
See her sleeping, stark and cold,
Still in that enchantment's hold.

From her lids his birds of spring
Fan the snowflakes with their wing;
Out of deathly dreams and chill
Ooze the teardrops, melting still.

(O. ELTON)

I HEAR the stern decree: I bow to what is fated;
    Resistance, long ago, I told my heart was vain;
Yet, ere that sacrifice in tears be consummated,
    Why must love utterly fall silent, and refrain?

Let censure pass unheard; enjoy, the hour is fleeting;
    To-morrow's grim routine may be like yesterday's;
Meantime, prolong the kiss, the passionate glances meeting,
    While hope with fiery dreams presumptuously plays.

(O. ELTON)

NIKOLAI NEKRASOV
(1821–1877)

I THOUGHT on war with horrors rife,
Each victim new of battle sought,
Yet pitied neither friend nor wife
Nor pitied even those who fought.

Alas, for comfort comes to wife ;
Friend will forget his dearest friend.
Yet somewhere breathes one only life
That will remember till its end.

Hypocrisies surround our days,
Our life of prose and mean career ;
One only meets my searching gaze,
One only true and sacred tear —

The tear from mothers' hearts that cry,
Forgetting not their sons who lie
On battle's bloody cornfield — dead,
As willow weeps nor lifts its head
Of downcast boughs towards the sky.

(SIR CECIL KISCH)

HAPPY that easy-tempered bard I call
Whose nature's rich in feeling, poor in gall.
To him the friends of quiet elegance
The cordial hand of fellowship advance ;
Soft as the rumour of the waves to hear,
The noise of general interest lulls his ear ;
Smiling and smiled upon, he lives without
The torture of creative souls — self-doubt.
And loving ease, accepting peace for truth,
Abominating satire's whetted tooth,
His dilettante lyre not rudely loud
Wields undisputed empire o'er the crowd.

Awe-struck at his gigantic powers of mind
No room for slight or slander can they find ;
And each contemporary critic vies
To rear his monument before he dies.

   But if some nobler spirit shall dare to point
And teach the times that they are out of joint,
Their passions and their follies dare to unmask —
What sentence must he hope ?   What pardon ask ?
With feasts of hate his heart he first equips,
With edge of mockery arms his pilgrim lips,
And walks alone upon a path of thorns
Thrumming a lyre of chastisements and scorns.

   Yet hours will come when even the mightiest
Craves for a friend to assure, a sign to attest,
The sterling truth which all refuse for base :
But he, whom scandal hunts from place to place,
Where shall he, dogged by that reproachful train,
Those dear salutes of approbation gain ?
Worth, which no tongues of common praise requite,
Finds in the screech of irritated spite
A sweeter meed than praise could e'er indite.

   Now faint with disbelief, now clear by faith,
The vision of his calling, like a wraith,
Guides him to preach evangels of goodwill . . .
And preaching, pass for renegado still.
For not a word he utters, but thereby
The number of his foes shall multiply :
Till all together, empty heads and wise,
Are fain to brand their mark between his eyes,
And let the Public read upon his forehead,
" He speaks the thing that is.   His mind is horrid."

   And so 'tis curses here and curses there —
And till they see his corpse no soul will care
To look what he's achieved, or estimate
How greatly he must love who did so hate.

(J. S. Phillimore)

INNOKENTI ANNENSKY
(1856–1909)

October Myth

'TIS too much, the blind man's tread,
And I can no longer bear it.
All night long above my head
Stumbling on the roof I hear it.

Are they mine, the scalding tears,
In my heart? There is no telling.
Or, with question that none hears,
Come they from his blind eyes welling?

Down wan cheeks that sorrows stain,
From dim eyeballs come they swimming,
Down the dripping window-pane
In the lonely midnight brimming?

(C. M. BOWRA)

Poppies

THE gay day flames. The grass is still.
Like greedy impotence, poppies rise,
Like lips that lust and poison fill,
Like wings of scarlet butterflies.

The gay day flames. . . . The garden now
Is empty. Lust and feast are done.
Like heads of hags, the poppies bow
Beneath the bright cup of the sun.

(C. M. BOWRA)

FEDOR SOLOGUB
(1863–1927)

I CAME. Cool are the meadows here.
  I came from far to greet her,
And my death will be light to bear,
  Than poison sweeter.

My drooping head to grief I give.
  The dew falls on the grasses.
And still I breathe. And still I live.
  So soon life passes.

Dusk comes, and silently comes she,
  Her footsteps softly falling,
And she is singing songs to me,
  To freedom calling.

I came. And she is very near.
  Her eyes soothe all who greet her,
And my death will be light to bear,
  Than poison sweeter.
(C. M. Bowra)

THE stifling day was harsh and hot ;
Though silent, it is not yet dead,
And the exhausted dusk has not
Lost in the shadows all its red.
Already, almost visible,
A sickle moon has risen high.
With breath as of a magic spell
The outspread fields in silence lie.
And everything now seems to say
That holy, happy wonders start
In silent skies, vales far away,
And in the trembling of my heart.
And like a far bell's quiet tone,
The breath foretells that peace is nigh.
The solitary sickle moon
Has risen over earth on high.
(C. M. Bowra)

KONSTANTIN BALMONT
(1867–1939)

Morning

FROM the peaks a vulture of the mountains cries.
On the wind to me that dying cadence flies.
Not alone I saw the spring day's dawn arise.

Now the sun has spread his pointed beams of light ;
They have turned to crimson, and their flames are bright,
And to them in answer streams sing on the height.

Oh but how much strength and how much love abound !
Oh how softly swoons the mountain grass around !
Distant friend, about thee is my spirit wound.

I look down the valley from the mountain's brow ;
Flowers burst to bud with thoughts of passion now.
In the world the sun is, in my heart art thou.

(C. M. BOWRA)

Under Sea

IT is good under sea where trees grow.
Light is pale, and the sea depths are dumb.
Only shadows of ships come and go,
And to us the sea's waves never come.

The sea trees are unmoved and serene,
And unmoved and serene their increase.
Not a sound in their shadow of green,
And they blossom in silence and peace.

The sea floor has no echoes below,
And its grass by no ripple is tossed.
And for us who loved once, long ago,
All remembrance of earth's speech is lost.

Coloured rocks, and the sand, and astray
Phantom fishes that pass silently.
All life's passion and pain far away,
It is good to be drowned in the sea.

(C. M. BOWRA)

VYACHESLAV IVANOV
(1866–   )

Now the golden leaves have been beggared,
And piercing the shadows of autumn
Shines the bright, blue stillness of heaven.
The wood with its delicate columns
Has turned to a carved, stone cathedral ;
Among the white pillars mist rises.
On its doors transparent and splendid
Hangs a curtain, like nets of God's fishers
All broken and torn by their catches,
Or like to your sanctified tatters
Before the white porch of a temple,
Songs golden and poverty-stricken !

(C. M. Bowra)

Funerals

Of funerals the saddest,
My friends, is that which buries
A love without fulfilment.
Then two the soul must bury,
The soul of its belovèd
And its own soul, a stranger.
And when the flames have caught them,
A third soul enters, living,
A yoke laid on its pinions ;
Him do the lips of lovers
Call in their kisses " Eros "
And gods " The Resurrector ".

(C. M. Bowra)

MAXIM GORKY
(1868–1936)

Song of the Hawk

HIGH in the mountains,
In a wet valley,
A serpent settled,
Motionless, knotted,
And looked out seaward.

High in the heaven
The sun was shining ;
With heat the mountains
Breathed to the heaven,
And waves lashed loudly
On rocky ledges.

But in the valley,
In spray and darkness,
A stream came hurtling
To the sea's water,
Made the rocks thunder.

All white with foaming,
Grey-coloured, mighty,
It roared past mountains
And hurried seaward
In angry passage.

Then in that valley,
Where the snake rested,
A hawk from heaven
Fell, with breast gleaming
And blood-stained feathers.

Short cries repeating,
To the earth fallen,
His breast he battered
In helpless anger
On hard rock-ridges.

The snake was frightened,
Slipped away quickly,
But saw the bird had
Life left for only
Two or three minutes.

So to the stricken
Bird he crept nearer,
And hissing at him
Straight in his eyes said :
" Now you are dying ! "
" Yes, I am dying,"
The hawk made answer,
And deeply sighed he :
" I have lived nobly,
I have fought bravely,
And looked on heaven.
You have not seen it,
Though it is near you,
Miserable beggar ! "

" Nay, what is heaven ?
An empty region !
How can I creep there ?
It's fine for me here,
It's warm and wet here."
So the snake answered.
The bird of freedom
Smiled in his spirit
Over the foolish
Words of the serpent,
And so he pondered :
" Flying or crawling,
The end is certain. . . .
All in the earth lie,
And all become dust."

Then the hawk daring
Suddenly started,
Raised himself slightly,
And round the valley
His glances wandered.

Through the grey boulders
The water trickled,
And it was stifling
In the hot valley —
Smell of corruption.
Then the hawk cried out
In pain and weakness,
His strength collecting :
" If I could only
Soar to the heaven !
I'd squeeze my foeman
To my breast wounded
And suffocate him
In my blood streaming.
Oh, bliss of battle ! "

" I should inhabit
Heaven," the snake thought,
" And pass delighted
Days in such doings
As now he sighs for."

To the free bird then
He made proposal :
" You will go forward
To the ravine's edge,
Fling yourself forward.
Maybe your wings will
Carry you upward,
And you'll live longer
For a brief season
In your own region."
And the hawk trembled,
And crying proudly
Went to the rock-edge,
Gliding with talons
On the wet boulders.

On he made headway,
Spreading his wings out,
All his breast panting,

Cast his eyes upward,
And then fell downward ;
Like a stone dropping,
Into the gully
Suddenly fell he,
Breaking his pinions,
Wrecking his feathers.

The swollen current
Laid hold upon him,
Washed the blood off him,
On its foam took him
And whirled him seaward.

The sea's great breakers
Bellowing sadly
Beat on the shingle . . .
And the bird's body
Could be seen nowhere
In the sea spaces.

Long in the valley
The snake lay thinking
How the bird perished,
How he loved heaven ;
Then turned his glances
All round the valley
Where eyes play ever
With dreams of pleasure.

" What did he see there,
The hawk who perished,
In that waste desert,
Dayless, unbounded ?
Why do those like him,
The hawk who perished,
Trouble their spirit
With this strong passion
For flight in heaven ?
What brightness find they ?
If I could only
Once understand it

And fly in heaven
For a few moments ! "
Words turned to action.
In a ring circling
In the air spun he
And, a thin ribbon,
Glittered in sunlight.

Born to go creeping
Take wing he cannot. . . .
Of that unmindful
On the stones fell he,
But no hurt suffered
And burst out laughing :
" See the enchantment
Of flight in heaven !
It lies in tumbling !
Birds, silly creatures !
Knowing the earth not,
Longing for heaven,
They hurry upward,
Aloft towards it,
And seek to live there
In a hot desert.
'Tis only desert,
'Tis only light there,
Nothing to keep life
For a live body.

Why all this pride, then ?
Why these reproaches ?
Why, save to shelter
With its protection
Their senseless longing
And hide behind it
Their great unfitness
For life and action ?
Birds, silly creatures !
I am no longer
Tricked and persuaded
By their wild speeches !

I see it all now !
I've seen the heaven,
I've flown to heaven,
Taken its measure,
Learned about falling,
But not been broken ;
Only more strongly
I trust myself now.
Let them who cannot
Love earth below here,
Live in illusions.
I know the whole truth.
As for their challenge,
I disbelieve it.
Earth is creation,
Earth's life sufficient."

He curled himself up
On a stone ball-wise,
Proud, self-contented. . . .
The sea was shining,
With light resplendent,
And the waves fiercely
Beat on the beaches.

With lion bellow
Songs rang and thundered
The proud bird's glory,
And the rocks shivered
Beneath their onslaught ;
And the skies shivered
From the fierce singing :
" Of gallant frenzy
We sing the glory !
In gallant frenzy
Is life's true wisdom.
O hawk undaunted,
Fighting your foeman
In blood you perished. . . .
A time is coming
When blood shed by you

Will burn and glitter
And flame like flashes
Into life's darkness,
And many gallant
Hearts will be flaming,
Frenzied and thirsty,
O world, for freedom !
Though you have perished,
In songs of courage
And in brave spirits
You will be always
A living pattern,
A haughty summons
To life, to freedom !
Of gallant frenzy
We sing the glory ! ”

(C. M. Bowra)

ALEXANDER BLOK
(1880–1921)

I SEEK salvation.
My beacons burn on every high hill —
Across night's wide domain you see them flare,
But the Soul's glance in me is brighter still :
Thou art afar . . . but art thou there ?
    I seek salvation.

Triumphantly the starry chorus fill
The heavens with song — and men seek my damnation.
I lit my fires for thee on every hill ;
Thou art — imagination ?
    I seek salvation.

Weary of singing, the heavenly choir is still ;
Now passes night, now flees all hesitation.
Thou comest now from that far shining hill.
I longed for thee.   Towards thee I stretched my will.
    In thee is my salvation.

                    (V. DE S. PINTO)

EVENING mist on the land was lying,
    When in a whirl of wind and flame
From the Koran a winged angel flying
    To my poor lifeless spirit came.
My mind was feeble and longed for slumber,
    But my spirit was strong and flew. . . .
Round me rustled wings without number ;
    I heard strange voices singing too.

                    (V. DE S. PINTO)

I PLANTED my bright Paradise
And built high walls around in order ;
My Mother seeks her son in skies
Of azure by th' enchanted border.

" Where are thou, dearest son of mine ? "
Silence. Inside the sunlight thickens
The grapes and slowly, surely quickens
My valley's Paradisal wine.

Lightly my Mother's footstep falls
Upon my garden, in my bowers,
And, careful not to crush the flowers,
" Where art thou, son ? " again she calls.

And all is still. Can she surmise
How the heart ripens unattended,
How other joys for him are ended
Who tastes the wine of Paradise ?

(C. M. Bowra)

GLORY and gallant deeds and fame forgetting,
I lived awhile in lands of misery,
And saw your picture in simple setting
Across the table shining back to me.

But time passed by, and from my home you wandered ;
I flung the holy ring to nightly space.
Your fortunes to another you surrendered,
And I forgot the beauty of your face.

The swarms of days accursed came on me falling ;
My life was rent by passion and by wine.
Before God's shrine I knelt, your face recalling,
And cried to you, as youth that once was mine.

I cried to you ; no word came back replying.
And tears I shed, but still you did not come.
In a blue cloak you wrapped yourself up, sighing,
And on a rainy night you went from home.

I know not what a refuge may enfold you,
My darling and my sweet one, in your pride ;
I slumber deep and in my dreams behold you,
In that blue cloak in the wet night outside.

No use to dream of days renowned or tender ;
All now is finished, youth has had its day.
That face that shone once in its simple splendour
Across the table, I have pushed away.

(C. M. Bowra)

PIPES on the bridge struck up to play ;
Flowers tipt the apple-spray ;
And one green star, aloft, away,
Uplifted by an angel, lay.
Miraculous, on the bridge to-day
To look into the deeps that stay
Aloft, so far away !

The pipe sings loud, the star climbs high.
(Now shepherd, homeward ply !)
Beneath the bridge the wave sings by : —
" Ah, look, how fast the waters go !
(Forget for ever all thy care)
Thou never saw'st so deep a flow,
So lucid, anywhere. . . .
Or listenedst to such deeps below
Of silence, anywhere. . . .

Ah, look, how fast the waters flow ;
When didst thou dream it ? Dost thou know ? "

(O. Elton)

My darling, be brave,
    Come, live with me :
I am the white cherry bough
    That sways over thee.

I am the shining green star,
    In the East I abide :
I am the cold billow washing
    The ship's iron side.

I am the free water-nymph
  Diving under the stream :
To be free and together,
  Ah, what a sweet dream !

And in the dark night
  So gently to die
And look at each other
  With cold glassy eye.

                   (V. DE S. PINTO)

WHAT long-forgotten gleam is this ?
  An instant, through the violinning
  I catch a different strain beginning !
That low, deep voice of hers it is.

— Of her, my friend of old, replying
  To my first love ; and I recall
  It always on the days when fall
The snowstorms, blusterously flying ;

When traceless melts the past, and when
  'Tis only alien passions tell me,
Tell me a little, now and then,
  Of happiness that once befell me.

                      (O. ELTON)

A SEASON comes, a day comes, when
Snows burst into the heart and quiver ;
No gentle voices can deliver
It, nor still hours of labour then.

A bird alarmed and shyly darting
You fly, but dawn is red with blood. . . .
With anguish, passion, fever starting
Love's lunacy comes unwithstood.

Then half the heart is a dark thunder,
And all below is dead and dumb.
And it that was before so tender
Strange and another has become.

Stifling and dark and gaily playing
It gasps and almost breathes no more,
In all the other's will obeying,
The soul that was so proud before.

(C. M. BOWRA)

Ravenna

INTERRED in ages past thou keepest
    All frail and momentary things,
And like a child, Ravenna, sleepest
    Beneath Eternity's drowsed wings.

No slaves, with their mosaics loaded,
    Now pass the Roman gate ; and all
The gilding burns away, corroded,
    On the basilica's cold wall.

The rude sepulchral arches weather
    Beneath the ooze's lingering kiss ;
O'er coffined queen and monk together
    For ever creeps the verdigris.

Dumb are the burial-halls, and shady
    And chill their doors, lest Galla rise.
The very stones, that sainted lady
    Would calcine with her sombre eyes.

Forgot are wars, wiped out for ever
    Their trail of blood, their harms, their rage.
Placidia, wake not ! chant thou never
    The passions of a vanished age !

Far out the sea has ebbed ; a riot
    Of roses clasps the wall, in bloom ;
The storms of life must not disquiet
    Theodoric, dreaming in his tomb.

The people, and the homes they sat in,
  The vine-hung wastes, are graves. Alone,
The lettered bronze, the sovereign Latin,
  Rings like a trumpet on the stone ;

And only the Ravenna lasses
  With mute fixed looks, forbear to hide
A rare, a shy regret that passes,
  For that still unreturning tide.

Sole, nightly o'er those valleys bending,
  The wraith of Dante aquiline
Counts on the Future, to me sending
  His song of the New Life divine.

(O. Elton)

THE hours and days and years are fleeting.
I wish to drive a dream away,
Give men and nature open greeting
And dissipate my twilit day.

There something flaps. Its glitter teases,
(So shadows on the steps at night
Make silhouettes when winter freezes,
Then quickly fade away from sight).

A sword ! It's gone. It was not needed.
What made my arm grow weak and swoon ?
I call to mind pearls finely threaded
That gleam at night beneath the moon.

The frost is sorrowful and sickly,
The sea is smooth beneath the snow. . . .
Eyes flash a shining horror quickly,
An ancient horror — let me know.

A voice ? Not that. What was it falling ?
No dream, no phantom. Far from here
It rang, then faded, ceased from calling
And left the earth to disappear

And die. But lips again were singing,
And hours, or years, came passing by. . . .
(Only the telegraphs were ringing
On wires beneath the darkened sky.)

Then suddenly with clear insistence
A voice I know and understand
Cries " Ecce Homo ! " from the distance.
Down falls my sword, trembles my hand.

With stifling silk tied round me, fearful
Lest blood should gush forth from the vein,
I waited dutiful and cheerful
And took no weapon up again.

Now comes the hour. Of old I know it,
Who thought, " I am no servant, no ! "
I tear the flowered sling and throw it.
Gush forth, blood, and make red the snow !

(C. M. Bowra)

Dance of Death

It's hard for a dead man to play at passion,
As though he lived among men living here ;
But he must mingle with the rank and fashion
Nor let his rattling bones stop his career.

Live men are sleeping when the dead man rises ;
His thoughts are black as the white nights are long.
He goes to bank or senate or assizes,
And quill-pens scratch for him a triumph-song.

All through the day the dead man goes on writing,
Till, when the office needs him there no more,
He wags his rump, under his breath reciting
A bawdy story to a senator.

The evening rain has smeared with dirty liquor
Humans and houses, all things dank and drab.
The dead man goes to where the filth is thicker
And whirls off in a shaky taxi-cab.

A crowded ball-room, pillars all about it, —
His evening clothes are in the smartest style.
His idiot host and hostess do not doubt it,
And he is welcomed with a gracious smile.

The dull official day has made him weary, —
But who can hear his rattle, with that band ?
To prove that he's alive he must be cheery
And heartily shakes each one by the hand.

But who's that by the column in the distance ?
His eyes meet hers, for like him she is dead.
Behind their talk of commonplace existence
You hear the real words in what is said.

" O weary friend, by no one am I greeted.
O weary friend, the cold grave knows me too.
It is midnight." " But you have not entreated
Her for a waltz. She is in love with you."

And over there, with all her senses reeling
For him, for him, with all her blood on fire,
A maiden waits, her lovely eyes revealing
The senseless ecstasy of live desire.

To her he whispers things that do not matter,
Words that enchant the living with their charm ;
He sees her head towards her shoulder flutter,
He sees the rosy brightness of her arm.

With more than human malice, in her ear
He pours the poison of his witty prattling.
" He is so clever, and he thinks me dear ! "
But strange, uncanny noises she can hear
When bones on bones are rattling.

(C. M. Bowra)

Night : the street, a foolish lamp giving
    A dingy light, a druggist's store :
For a quarter of a century go on living.
    No escape. All will be as before.

You die : afresh you start life boldly.
Just as before, each detail repeat.
Night : the canal rippling so coldly,
The druggist's store, the lamp, the street.

(V. DE S. PINTO)

The New America

O DAY of gladness, O feast of glory,
Thou star that lurk'st behind a cloud,
To a wild dance music moves thy story,
My native land, fateful and proud !

Behind forests and steppes and snows unsleeping,
Thy face is ever hidden from me,
Only thy terrible expanses sweeping,
Unmeasured, vast like an endless sea.

Into a monstrous snowdrift flying
I sit on a sledge that crazily spins,
And see thee in thy rich tomb lying,
Old squalid Russia of the Finns !

You dressed yourself like an old psalm-singing
Woman, you acted a life of prayer !
Murmur of liturgies, church bells ringing,
And crosses, crosses everywhere.

Through incense steaming blue and rosy
Sometimes I saw your authentic grace,
Under the Moscow kerchief's posy
There lurked no aged, fasting face.

Through genuflections, tapers that gutter —
Prayers, endless prayers to God's holy name,
Through the everlasting priestly mutter
I saw your cheeks like a living flame.

Still onward, onward, always raving,
The storm-winds over the black earth roll,
The wayside bush in the tempest waving
Is fluttering like a deacon's stole.

74

At length beside the river full-flowing,
    Where bows to the ground the feather-grass grey,
A burning smell on the breeze comes blowing
    And I hear strange hootings far away. . . .

Is it a Polish host returning,
    Or Tartar hordes to rob and kill,
Or the turbaned Turk, destroying and burning,
    Who wreaks on the steppe his cruel will?

No, here is no ancient princely banner,
    No water of Don from helmets poured,
No fair Varangian in a servile manner
    Bowing her head to a Polish lord.

No gay flags on the steppes are flowering,
    No pennons in the breezes stream. . . .
I see black factory chimneys towering,
    And everywhere the hooters scream.

Path of your steppes, without limit your floor is . . .
    Steppes, winds, and still winds that nothing can
        bound. . . .
I see huge factories with many stories,
    And workers' cities clustering round.

In the empty wilds, the homeless spaces,
    Another thou art, yet ever the same,
Showing now a new face of thy many faces,
    A new vision leaping like a flame.

Black coal, Messiah subterranean,
    Thy Tsar, thy bridegroom in his pride,
Now roars his songs from depths vulcanian;
    Thou fear'st them not, O Russia, his bride!

Now crackles the coal, now the salt whitens,
    I hear molten iron hiss from afar,
Now over thy empty steppes there brightens,
    My America, my new-risen star!

                                        (V. DE S. PINTO)

75

THE white flag I never surrendered,
Though deafened by enemies' calls.
On journeys at night-time you wandered ;
I was with you, alone on the walls.

Yes, the fated night journeys that took you
Led apart and then joined us once more ;
And, my Russia, we never forsook you,
But came back from an alien shore.

The mounds of our brothers, the crosses,
That is where you are, Peace, — in the grave.
And the soldiers' sad melody tosses
To us from afar like a wave.

All is silent and empty beside us,
Friend and foe in death's dream, but above
Rises Bethlehem's bright star to guide us
And burns with a flame like my love.

(C. M. BOWRA)

The Twelve

I

BLACK dusk growing,
Snow falls white.
Wind, wind blowing !
On his legs a man can't stand upright.
Wind, wind blowing,
Through the whole creation going !

The wind twists and twirls
The white snow.
There is ice below ;
Heavy, slippery, —
If you try to go,
Down you fall — what a pity !

From building to building see
Stretched a great string,
From it a banner swing :
" All Power to the Constituent Assembly ! "
A weeping old woman has scanned it,
She cannot understand it :
    " What's the use of all that stuff,
    That enormous notice there ?
To clothe a whole people it's enough,
    But all go unshod and bare."

The old woman, like a hen,
Staggers along across the piles of snow.
    " O Mother who intercedest for men,
    The Bolsheviks drive us below ! "

The wind pierces ;
Sharper the frost grows.
At the street-corner the bourgeois'
Coat-collar hides his nose.

Who is that with hair fluttering ?
Under his voice muttering :
    " All is betrayed !
    Russia exists no more ! "
He must be a writer by trade
    Or an orator.

Another, long-skirted,
Lurks behind the snow.
Why are you down-hearted,
Comrade priest, now ?

Think how marched your swaying
Paunch in front of you,
With a cross displaying
Light the whole land through.

A lady in a lambskin coat
And her friend have a chat :
" Oh, the tears, the tears we shed . . ."
    Then end to end, pat,
She slips and falls down flat.

Tut, tut,
Lift her up.

The wild wind hurts,
Malignant, gay,
It flutters skirts
Of the passers-by,
Shakes, quakes and makes fly
The great placard away :
" All Power to the Constituent Assembly ! "
And voices float by. . . .

. . . " We held our committee . . .
In that part of the city . . .
Passed conclusions
And resolutions . . .
Ten for an hour, twenty-five for the night . . .
To take less isn't right. . . .
Come to bed, mate."

The darkness grows,
The streets are dead.
A single beggar
Droops his head.
The wind's whistle blows.

Oh, poor fellow,
Come here.
Let's have a kiss.

Bread !
What's up there ?
Keep clear !

Black, black sky overhead.

Hate, sorrowful hate
Boils in the heart . . .
Black hate, holy hate. . . .
Comrade, keep smart,
Look straight !

78

II

The wind reels, the snow dances ;
A party of twelve men advances.

Black rifle-slings upon their backs,
And flame, flame, flame about their tracks.

With crumpled caps, lips smoking fags,
All should be branded as prison lags.

    Freedom, freedom, ha !
      But no Cross, aha !
        Tra-ta-ta.

It's cold, comrades, it's cold.

" Vanya and Katya wet their throats."
" Her stockings are packed with Kerensky notes."

" Now Vanya's rich and prosperous."
" He joined up, though he was one of us."

" Vanya, son of a bitch, bourgeois,
If you kiss my girl and get off with her — ! "

    Freedom, freedom, ha !
      But no Cross, aha !
      Vanya and Katya are together —
      What are they doing together ?
        Tra-ta-ta.

With flame, flame, flame about their tracks,
And rifles slung upon their backs.

Revolutionaries, mind you keep
In step. The enemy does not sleep.

Don't shrink, comrade. Get your rifle out ;
Give Holy Russia a taste of shot,

79

The wooden land,
Where the poor huts stand,
And her rump so grand !

Aha, but no Cross !

III

When our boys joined up to fight,
To be soldiers with the Reds,
To be soldiers with the Reds,
And lay down their frenzied heads —

Ah, a bitter bitterness,
A sweet life we've won,
With a tattered overcoat
And an Austrian gun.

All the bourgeois will despair
When we set the world on fire,
Set the world on fire — in blood —
Send Thy blessing on us, God !

IV

Snow eddies, the coachman cries ;
Vanya past with Katya flies,
And the electric lamp's light shifts
On the carriage-shafts.
Ho, ho, bow low !

He, in soldier's overcoat,
Twists the black moustache about
On his idiotic face.
Watch him smile on her,
Try his style on her.

That's your Vanya, broad of back,
That's your Vanya — talk's his knack.
Silly Katya he embraces,
Shows her all his paces.

Into his her face she shows,
Bares her teeth in pearly rows. . . .
    Ah, my Katya, Katya mine,
    Your fat face is fine.

V

Katya, on your neck a gash is
From my knife, and does not heal.
Underneath your breast my slashes,
Katya, left another weal.

    Dance, then, dance for me !
    Your fine feet are good to see.

White lace underclothes you kept then, —
Walk the streets and play your part, —
With the officers you slept then, —
Be a tart, then, be a tart.

    Well, well, be a tart.
    In my breast leaps up my heart.

Once an officer preferred you —
And my knife was in his flesh.
Ah, you pox, has that not stirred you ?
Is the memory not fresh ?

    Well, refresh me too !
    I should like to sleep with you.

In grey gaiters you went walking ;
Fancy chocolate was your style.
With cadets you did the talking ;
Now you go with rank and file ?

    Well, well, sin away.
    It will keep the spirit gay.

VI

Again at a gallop the coachman flies,
And charges past with yells and cries.

Halt there, you ! Halt ! Now, Andrew, mind,
And, Peter, follow up behind.

Trac-tararac-tac-tac-tac-tac,
The snow whirls skyward in his track.

The coachman flies, and Vanya too.
Take your aim on them, all of you.

Trac-tararac. You soon will learn
Not to take your friend's girl for a turn.

. . . .

The blackguard's gone. Well, just you wait.
To-morrow I shall put it straight.

But where is Katya, where ? Dead . . . dead. . . .
A bullet shot her through the head.

Do you like that, Katya ? Not a sound.
Lie, carrion, on the snowy ground.

Revolutionaries, mind you keep
In step. The enemy does not sleep.

VII

On the twelve men march again,
Every rifle in its place.
Only the poor murderer's pain
Drives the colour from his face.

Faster, ever faster, shuffles
On his hurried step away ;
And his neck a wrapper muffles.
Nothing now can make him gay.

" Why are you down-hearted, chum ?
Why, friend, do you feel so low ? "
" Peter, why are you so glum ?
Does your Katya sting you so ? "

" Oh, my comrades, friends of mine,
How I used to love that lass !

82

Nights of darkness, nights of wine,
Drunkenly we used to pass.

" Ah, her eyes that flared afar,
Flaming with a crazy light !
Ah, the little crimson star
By her shoulder on the right !
Stupidly I murdered her,
Murdered her from raging spite."

" Stop that silly tune, will you ?
You're a woman, you old fool.
What is it you think you do,
Turning inside out your soul ?
Give your pride a thought or two,
What about your self-control ?

" This is not a time to spare
For your troubles without end.
We shall have a load to bear
Heavier than this, my friend."

So his pace poor Peter slows,
No more leaves the rest behind.

Proudly up his head he throws,
Is his happy self again.

Well, well,
Fun won't send you down to Hell.

Lock up all the handsome homes !
Now the time of looting comes.

Fling the cellars open, all !
'Tis the beggars' carnival !

VIII

Oh, miserable misery !
Black boredom fills me
And kills me.

Long hours on watch
I shall wait, I shall wait.

Now I shall scratch
My old pate, my old pate.

Sunflower-seed
I shall split, I shall split.

With my knife-blade
I shall slit, I shall slit.

Clear out, bourgeois, off with you !
  I shall drink in blood
  To my love's hot flood
  And your eyes' black hood.

Give rest, O Lord, to the soul of Thy servant.

    Misery.

IX

On all the Nevski buildings peace.
The city's din has died away.
Comrade, there are no more police.
Without a drop to drink, be gay !

The bourgeois, where the roads divide,
Stands with his nose sunk in his fur ;
And, hairy, shivers at his side,
With drooping tail, a poor whipped cur.

Like the dog, stands the bourgeois, hungry,
A silent question to the sky ;
The old world, like a homeless mongrel,
With tail between its legs stands by.

X

Wind grows stronger — what a wind !
  Oh, the wind, the wind !

Hardly can a friend see friend
Following four steps behind.

Black the snow that twists and twirls,
Like a column upward curls.

" Saviour, what a storm it is ! "
" Peter, don't talk stuff like this.
What can all that nonsense do,
Those gold images, for you ?
What is it you talk about ?
Try to reason, think it out.
Stains of blood upon your hand
Come from your loved Katya, friend."
" Comrades, watch your step.   I fear
Sleepless enemies are near."

March on, march on, march on,
Workers in unison !

XI

On without God's holy name they swing ;
Still the twelve go marching on,
Ready for anything,
Pitying none.

Loudly the steel rifles blaze
Volleys on the unseen foe.
By deserted passage-ways
Through the ceaseless storm they go.
Heavy boots are hard to raise
From the downy drifts of snow.

In their eyes shaking
The red flag blows.

Loud the unbreaking
March onward goes.

Over there waking
Are brutal foes.

In their eyes the wind alight
    Day and night
    Stops for none.

    On, workers, on
    In unison.

XII

On with sovereign steps they go. . . .
" Who is hiding there ? Get out ! "
Nothing but the gusts that blow,
Flapping a red flag about.

There's an icy drift ahead.
" Who is in the drift ? Get out ! "
Only a poor dog, unfed,
Hobbles on behind the rout.

" Off, you mangy beast, or itch
With a taste of bayonet.
Old world, like a scabby bitch,
I shall flay you ! Out you get ! "

It shows teeth in wolfish grin,
Follows tail down, does not care.
Frozen dog, dog without kin.
" Answer quickly, who goes there ? "

" Who flaps that red flag ahead ? "
" Can you see him ? What a night ! "
" Who is it with silent tread
Lurks about us, out of sight ? "

" We shall get you, all the lot.
Best give in while breathing still !
Friend, I'll put you on the spot ;
Get out, or I shoot to kill."

Trac-tac-tac, and nothing after ;
Echoes from the buildings blow.

Nothing but the wind's long laughter
Sings in answer on the snow.

    Trac-tac-tac,
    Trac-tac-tac.

On they march with sovereign tread,
With a starving dog behind,
With a blood-red flag ahead —
In the storm where none can see,
From the rifle bullets free,
Gently walking on the snow,
Where like pearls the snowflakes glow,
Marches rose-crowned in the van
Jesus Christ, the Son of Man.

                 (C. M. Bowra)

ANDREI BELY
(1880–1934)

Bright Death

THE heavy and glittering goblet
Is emptied.   The earth has gone under.
All downward has fallen.   Beneath me
The coldness of space and of ether.
But in space immemorial rises
My glittering goblet, the Sun.

I look and see under my footsteps
The rivers, the forests, the valleys
Sink down to the depths, to the distance ;
But a cloud has blown into my eyelids
With mist, and it floats away downward,
Its gossamer glistening golden.

The landscape of noontide has faded,
The stars of the noontide look into
My spirit, and each word of " Welcome "
With radiance soundlessly glimmers :
" The time of long wandering over,
You wake in your own country.   Welcome."

Hour following hour in procession,
And century century, — smiling
I lift up in space immemorial
My glittering goblet, the Sun.

(C. M. BOWRA)

Russia

WAIL, element tossed by the tempest
In pillars of thunderous fire :
O Russia, my Russia, my Russia,
Rage, rage, burn me up in thy pyre !

88

For into thy fated destruction,
Thy shrouded abysses, is borne
A host of winged spirits like angels
Whose dreams are as bright as the morn.

Then weep not, but kneel in devotion
And pray in the hurricane's blaze,
The thundering chorus of seraphs,
The torrent of cosmical days.

The dry, barren wastes of dishonour,
The seas of unquenchable tears,
From light in His look, though He speak not,
Will sparkle when Christ's face appears.

Leave Heaven its girdle of Saturn,
Its milky and silvery ways ;
And seethe, blaze like light in the tempest,
Earth-ball, with thy fiery rays !

O element, fiery, blazing,
Rage, rage, let thy flames feed on me,
O Russia, my Russia, my Russia,
Messiah of days soon to be !

(C. M. BOWRA)

SERGEI GORODETSKY
(1884-   )

Spring in the Convent

BELLS and sighs, bells slowly tolling,
Bells and mourning, bells and dreams.
High and steep the hill-slopes rolling,
Green the sloping hillside gleams.
White the walls are bleached anew ;
So the Abbess bade them do.
At the gate on sentinel
Weeps a maid who tolls the bell.

Ah, the fields where I'll be free,
Ah, the road, the road for flight !
Bridge and clean fields waiting me,
Thursday's clean and holy light !

Ah, my light that brightly burned,
' Twas for him it died away.
I was faint, my breath returned
Hotter than my heart that day.

How I quavered, how I quivered
By the tall bridge parapet.
Flame of candles shook and shivered,
And our lips in kisses met.

Where art thou whom then I kissed ?
Darling, where art thou, so kind ?
Ah, the haze of spring, the mist,
Ah, for girlhood's quiet mind !

Bells and sighs, bells slowly tolling,
Bells and mourning, bells and dreams.
High and steep the hill-slopes rolling,
Green the sloping hillside gleams.
White the walls are bleached anew ;
So the Abbess bade them do,
Not in idleness to wait
At the convent gate.

(C. M. BOWRA)

VLADISLAV KHODASEVICH
(1885–1938)

WHAT is the use of time and rhyme ?
We live in peril, paupers all.
The tailors sit, the builders climb,
But coats will tear and houses fall.

And only seldom with a sob
Of tenderness I hear . . . oh, quite
A different existence throb
Through this mortality and blight.

Thus does a wife, when days are dull,
Place breathlessly, with loving care,
Her hand upon her body, full
Of the live burden swelling there.

(V. NABOKOV)

Stanzas

BRIGHTLY lit from above, I am sitting
In my circular room ; this is I —
Looking up at a sky made of stucco,
At a sixty-watt sun in that sky.

All around me, and also lit brightly,
All around me my furniture stands,
Chair and table and bed — and I wonder
Sitting there what to do with my hands.

Frost-engendered white feathery palm-trees
On the window-panes silently bloom ;
Loud and quick ticks the watch in my pocket
As I sit in my circular room.

Oh, the leaden, the beggarly bareness
Of a life where no issue I see !
Whom on earth could I tell how I pity
My own self and the things around me?

And then clasping my knees I start slowly
To sway backwards and forwards, and soon
I am speaking in verse, I am crooning
To myself as I sway in a swoon.

What a vague, what a passionate murmur
Lacking any intelligent plan ;
But a sound may be truer than reason
And a word may be stronger than man.

And then melody, melody, melody
Blends my accents and joins in their quest,
And a delicate, delicate, delicate
Pointed blade seems to enter my breast.

High above my own spirit I tower,
High above mortal matter I grow ;
Subterranean flames lick my ankles,
Past my brow the cool galaxies glow.

With big eyes, as my singing grows wilder,
With the eyes of a serpent maybe,
I keep watching the helpless expression
Of the poor things that listen to me.

And the room and the furniture slowly,
Slowly start in a circle to sail,
And a great heavy lyre is from nowhere
Handed by a ghost through the gale.

And the sixty-watt sun has now vanished,
And away the false heavens are blown ;
On the smoothness of glossy white boulders
This is Orpheus standing alone.

(V. Nabokov)

VIKTOR KHLEBNIKOV
(1885–1922)

Death Feast

STARK the row of corpses lies,
Songs of death have ceased to sound.
Soldiers wait with downcast eyes,
Airmen's shadows fleck the ground.

When the oak-wood pyre was made
Where the silent village ends,
" Glory be to God " we said,
Burned the bodies of our friends.

Are we men or spears of Fate,
All in that same, single hand ?
We know nothing.   For us wait
Distant trenches to be manned.

He who lives picks up the dead ;
Flaxen curls in dead men's hair.
Bodies on the wood are laid,
Russians keep the death feast there.

Black mist swells along the skies,
Black and thick and strong it swells.
We stand at the sacrifice ;
For the rite commands farewells.

By the mounds, the hundred lakes,
Many dead men's sticks displayed.
On the pile of harsh oak stakes
Russian bodies have been laid.

From the flesh of watchful dead
Don and Irtish rise and sweep.
The grey whirling mist has fled,
We remain and silence keep.

When the age-old oaken pyre
With its flames the mist has lit,
Vainly we our rifles fire,
Then together turn from it.

(C. M. Bowra)

NATIONS, years and every creature
In an endless river go,
As the passing waters flow.
In the subtle glass of nature
Stars are nets, and fishes we,
Gods the midnight's mystery.

(C. M. Bowra)

Liberty for All

IN a stormwind, single, undying,
All, all are for Liberty there !
On swans' wings the People are flying
To lift flags of work in the air.

Liberty flames on their faces, —
Fire set beside it is cold.
Who cares for old shapes on earth's places ?
New words shall their hunger unfold.

We march with songs that are burning,
Together to Liberty, on !
Though we die, we shall rise, and returning
Life shall revive what has gone.

We move on a journey enchanted,
And the loud marching rhythm we heed.
If the gods are in irons, undaunted
We shall see that the gods are freed !

(C. M. Bowra)

PRIEST of the springtime's Koran,
The cheerful priest, has stirred, —
My poplar, waiting early
To hear the morning's word.
When the fisher of the sun,
With casts of blue sky sweeping,
Has thrown his drag-nets out,
His cunning takes bulls roaring then,
And catches clouds still sleeping
And scent of snowy storm about.
O poplar fisherman,
You stand so green and tall
When you cast your nets of green
So many over all.
And lo ! the springtime's god
(A sturgeon astounded)
Lies on every boat
Amid the wet leaves' sheen.
The prayer, " Give us heaven "
Has opened lips of green.
With a god's catch that sevenfold yields
The giant poplar
With stroke of his horn
Strikes on the fields
With a wave of dark-blue vodka.

(C. M. BOWRA)

" I BELIEVE " sang the guns and the squares.
The cabman whips up his horses,
A coffin over his cart.
The image of revolt
Is revealed to the people.
You will not break it for a samovar.
The lord of pavements,
Painted in yesterday's blood,
In the thorns of new graves,
In the towels of shooting armies,
Looks from the squares at night

With death's big eyes,
A frame made of cobble-stones.
The image of a grim god
On the grey board
Set up by the hands of the days
Hangs over the capital :
Pray, ye people !
" Into the cellars, blue eyes !
Bullets and lashes for silent steps ! "
" Mother !
Is this the Terrible Judgment, mother ? "
" Sleep, my child, sleep,
Sleep, my child, sleep."

The broom of shots
With graveyards of money
Sweeps the streets —
A shaggy porter.
Bullets in pursuit, bullets in pursuit !
Three men sat down in a horse-tram,
Three men by leaden paths,
Turned to corpses.
A wild priest
With leaden curls
Sat down on a carpet of lead by the clouds.
In the graveyard's glow,
With sirens of factories wailing all night long
They have sought the face of the death-god.
Recognising acquaintances
People go to lift coffin-lids in lines on tip-toe.
Black streets.
The bullet like a gipsy from the camp
Dances and leaps at one's feet.
Like two gun-barrels
Are the eyes of him who sang
" From the foundations, but afterwards . . ."
Hands clutching iron rings,
The mob's glittering eyes underneath,
That laughter of death truly
Was the song of the floor of bullets.
A leaden wind,

An alarm in the dark night,
A gun rang into the valley of famine.
Windows form beautiful constellations,
Tears in the eyes are flights of bullets.
Steps on the glassy snow
Crunch crisply.
Behind a glass-grave a cat miaows :
" Tusa, tusa, tusa !
Men da da tsatso ! "

Bullets sang the street-camp.
Gusts of bullets
Blow in the ear of timid squares at night.
The sky has stuffed a sack with constellations.
The cloud of movement
Is whipped upward.

The poplar we felled just now, did it fall,
Did it crash, with a flutter of leaves ?
Or tired of bearing its top
Did it topple and bury many, ever so many ?

The poplar we felled, the poplar of salvoes,
Fell to the ground with leaves of lead
On the crowds, on the squares.
The poplar we felled, did it crash, did it fall
Suddenly on the crowd, did it fall on its face,
Covering with death's boughs the faces of many ?
Midnight screams of iron clang,
And stars' croak of the roofs of the death-house.
This night is black as a boot. . . .

Multitudes of stars, multitudes of birds
Suddenly rise in the air.
I have startled them.

(C. M. Bowra)

IT is time, it is time.
For you I'm
A star.

Grief to the sailor who has taken
The wrong angle of his ship
On a star :
He will be shattered on rocks,
On sand-banks below water.
Grief to you who have taken the heart's wrong angle
    on me.
You will be shattered on rocks,
And the rocks will smile
Over you,
As you used to smile
Over me.

(C. M. Bowra)

NIKOLAI GUMILEV
(1886–1921)

Memory

ONLY serpents change their outward skin
And permit their souls to grow and age.
But alas ! we men are not their kin, —
We discard our souls and not the cage.

Memory, who with a mighty hand
Lead our lives to some uncertain aim,
You will tell of those who lived and planned
In this shape of mine, before I came.

Number one : he loved the forest's dark,
Little wizard, thin and rather plain,
He knew every leaf and every bark,
And spoke magic words to stop the rain.

One wild dog and one wild tree he chose
As his friends, to live with him and die.
Memory you never would suppose,
Anyone could think that he was I.

And the second loved the southern wind,
Every noise, he said, was music sweet ;
He called life his girl who never sinned,
And the world — a mat beneath his feet.

I don't like him, nor his lust to shine
As a god for mortals to adore ;
It was he who pinned the poet's sign
On my modest dwelling's silent door.

I prefer that freedom's knight and bowman,
Sailor, roamer, hater of the crowds,
Who could watch the skies and read their omen,
Loved by oceans, envied by the clouds.

High upon the hills he built his tent,
And his mules were strong and unafraid ;
Like some fragrant wine he drank the scent
Of the land he was the first to tread.

Was it someone else, or was it he
(Memory, you weaken more and more),
Who exchanged his happy liberty
For the long awaited holy war ?

He knew nightmares in his endless quest,
Thirst and hunger in the roadless maze ;
But St. George touched twice his iron breast
Which a bullet never dared to graze.

I am now the stubborn architect,
Jealous of my predecessors' fame,
Trying arduously to erect
The Cathedral that shall burn like flame.

So my heart will burn and mind condemn,
Till the glorious day when there will stand
Golden walls of New Jerusalem
In the pastures of my native land.

Eerie winds will blow and bless the hour,
And the skies will send a blinding ray
From the planets, stars and suns in flower
In the gardens of the Milky Way.

Then a stranger with a hidden face
Will appear, and I shall know and break,
When I see the lion's kingly pace
And the eagle flying in his wake.

I shall know ; and where the road divides
I shall cry for help without reply. . . .
Only serpents can discard their hides, —
We must change our souls — and see them die.

(Y. Hornstein)

Reincarnation

So this is life ! Towns, deserts, ocean,
And being born, and being tossed, —
Reflection in a constant motion
Of things that are for ever lost.

The steed runs wild, the trumpets thunder,
And then — a pause in all the stress, —
A simple heart that stops in wonder
And lips that whisper happiness.

Once more, a fall, and more endeavour,
Despair and grief, and ecstasy,
And as before, and as for ever,
Towns, mountains, deserts and the sea.

When shall I waken, unencumbered,
Just I, as I began the ring,
A poor Hindu who calmly slumbered
One sacred evening by the spring ?

(Y. HORNSTEIN)

NIGHT was drawing in, and the fire was low.
He stood tall and sad in the dying glow,

Looking far beyond, with his eyes inert,
Speaking bitter words of the things that hurt.

" I have trailed through lands, fierce, unknown and vast ;
Eighty days on end did my journey last.

" We met bush and bog, and gigantic range,
And, at times, a town, distant, weird and strange.

" And on silent nights an uncanny roar
Reached us from those towns over marsh and moor.

" Giant trees we felled, through the bush we crept ;
Sometimes lions came close to where we slept.

" But my men were brave, and they used to rise
Catlike, and they aimed right between the eyes.

" I dug out a town, buried deep in sand,
Rivers bear my name in a distant land,

" And among the Lakes seven tribes preferred
To respect my law, to obey my word.

" But to-day I'm tired, listless and asleep,
Wounded is my soul, and the wound is deep.

" Even gushing winds will not ease my pain,
Even rushing seas will not break the chain. . . ."

Triumph in her eyes, as the light grew dim,
She was all the while listening to him.

(Y. HORNSTEIN)

Nature

THIS is the nature we behold,
The nature that our souls repel, —
Where scents of lilac in the fold
Mix with the marshes' putrid smell.

Where, like the jackals' hungry crowds,
The winds approach with mournful cries,
Where fleeting hosts of gaudy clouds
Disturb the emptiness of skies.

I see but shadows that mislead,
I see, bewildered and irate,
The scant diversity of seed
That God has deigned to dissipate.

O Earth, remember what you are,
Discard your beggarly attire,
And be yourself again — a star,
A flying star, imbued with fire !

(Y. HORNSTEIN)

The Giraffe

YOUR eyes are to-night so unusually thoughtful and sad,
Your hands are so thin round your knees, and your mouth will
    not laugh.
Listen : There roams, far away, by the waters of Chad,
An exquisite beast, the giraffe.

He moves like a ship in the vastness and stillness of space ;
Approaching, he seems to bewitch all the creatures around ;
His sails are inflated with winds of adventure and grace ;
He scarcely touches the ground.

He is kingly and straight, and his movements incredibly light ;
His skin is a play of the sun on the murmuring wave.
I know that the ostriches witness a wonderful sight,
When at nightfall he hides in his emerald cave.

I know many tales from the secret abodes of the earth,
Of Black Maidens and Chieftains, and orgies of passion and pain ;
But you have been breathing the fog from the day of your birth,
You would only believe in the rain.

So how can I tell you of gardens, magnolia-clad,
Of tropical scents, and of parrots that sparkle and laugh ?
You are crying ? Oh, listen, there roams, by the waters of Chad,
An exquisite beast, the giraffe.

(Y. HORNSTEIN)

The Forest

IN that forest whitish tree-trunks loom
Suddenly and ghostly through the gloom.

Crookéd roots in crippled embrace crawl
Like dead fingers up the churchyard wall.

Under foliage dense with stifling smell
Tribes of giants, dwarfs, and lions dwell.

And a seaman found there in the sand
Once a print of a six-fingered hand.

Through that jungle never yet did trail
Knights from France or of the Holy Grail.

Through that forest robbers never rode,
Nor did hermits seek there an abode.

Only once from there a woman came,
On a night of thunder, storm and flame,

Silver-crowned above her golden plait,
With the head and features of a cat ;

Her green eyes astir with mortal fright,
As she raved and trembled through the night.

And the village curate had not come
When she lay at sunrise cold and dumb.

All these happenings have taken place
At a time of which there is no trace.

All this happened, dearest, in a land
We shall never see or understand.

It is I who made it up, in dreams,
Looking at your braids — two fiery beams ;

Looking at your turquoise eyes that shone
Like that sickly oriental stone.

Think : Perhaps that forest is your shrine,
Or, perhaps, the tender love of mine.

Or, perhaps, we shall its thickets tread,
You and I, when we are gone and dead.

(Y. HORNSTEIN)

Trees

THE trees alone possess the gift sublime
Of perfect life, — not we who crawl and roam.
For on this earth, a sister of the stars,
We are on foreign soil and they — at home.

From autumn sunsets, cool and copper-tinged,
From amber-painted dawns, cold and serene,
The trees receive the glory of their hues,
And rise — a mighty people, free and green.

A Moses, surely, grows among the oaks,
A Mary among palms.   Perhaps they send
Their quiet greetings underground by springs,
Meandering through the dark from end to end.

Breaking the granite, cutting diamonds,
The springs converse and gossip, sing and roar ;
They carry stories of a broken elm
And of the splendour of a sycamore.

O for a land where also I were free
Not to regret, nor sing, nor weep, nor rhyme, —
Silently rising high and higher still,
Through fleeting ages to the end of time

(Y. HORNSTEIN)

Sonnet

I MUST be ill : my mind is dumb and bored
And there is naught that makes my heart respond.
I see in dreams a sparkling diamond
And streaming blood on a Mongolian sword.

I know of Tartars riding down the hills
And know — my ancestor, the slit-eyed Hun,
Has pierced my heart with all the savage ills
Of madness centuries ago begun.

And suddenly I see the walls of home
Recede, revealing seas of broken foam,
And granite rocks with crimson sunsets filled.

There was a town with cupolas of jade,
Folded in jasmin as in soft brocade,
There was a fight. . . . Ah, yes! and I was killed.

(Y. HORNSTEIN)

ANNA AKHMATOVA
(1889–   )

The Muse

THE Muse, my sister, gave me a look,
Her eyes were limpid and glowing,
And from me my golden ring she took,
First gift of the spring's bestowing.

Muse, you know well how happy are we,
Woman and widow and maiden.
Dead on the rack I would sooner be
Than with fetters like these be laden.

My future I shall not attempt to know
Or from daisy-buds guess the morrow ;
For everyone on this earth must go
Through love's sharp trial and sorrow.

In candle-light till the dawn is nigh
I sit, no one wanting or missing.
And no desire, no desire have I
To hear of another's kissing.

To-morrow the mirror will laugh and say
" Your eyes are not limpid or glowing ".
I shall answer it softly : " She took away
The gift that was God's bestowing ".

(C. M. BOWRA)

Now is woven in my dark tresses
A thread that is silvery pale —
No one knows what have been my distresses
But you only, my dumb nightingale.

With quick ears in the distances hearing
On soft leaves of the willow you stay,

Ruffle feathers, and breathe not, but peering
Wait for echoes of songs far away.

'Twas but lately, oh lately, that quiet
Was spread by the poplars around,
And you rang and you sang in a riot
Of delight in ineffable sound.

(C. M. BOWRA)

LIKE this, unto a wounded crane
The others cry : " To wing ! to wing ! "
When round them the autumnal plain
Is warm and mellowing.

So, weak and ill, I hear the call,
The whirr of golden wings,
That from the dense low clouds and all
The river thickets rings.

" 'Tis time to fly, 'tis time to fly
O'er river and o'er land.
Your hour of singing has gone by,
Nor have you strength your tears to dry,
So feeble is your hand."

(C. M. BOWRA)

To awake when dawn is breaking,
Just because joy stops me sleeping,
And to look out through the port-hole
Where the green waves beat outside,
Or on deck with the rain falling
To sit wrapped with furs around me,
Listen to the engine throbbing,
And to have no thoughts at all,
But expecting soon to meet him,
Him who is the star that guides me,
With the wind and salt spray blowing
To grow younger every hour.

(C. M. BOWRA)

IT is simple, it is easy,
Everyone can understand it;
Not the smallest love you bear me,
You will never long for me.
Why should I be full of longing
For a man who is a stranger?
Why should I kneel every evening
To put up a prayer for you?
Why should I forsake my comrade
And my curly-headed baby,
Throw away my native country
And the town that I love best,
And just like a dirty beggar
Wander through a foreign city?
Oh, how glad I am to think that
I shall soon be seeing you!

(C. M. BOWRA)

WINDS that bring the swans are racing,
Blood is dark upon the sky.
Anniversaries retracing
First days of your love come by.

All my sorceries you blasted;
Years, like water, flowed away.
Why are you by age not wasted
But the same as on that day?

Clearer your sweet voice comes ringing,
Though time's pinions circle now
Shades of snowy glory bringing
To the quiet of your brow.

(C. M. BOWRA)

Here I have waited, none with me,
To count my empty suns.
O friends who live in liberty,
My company of swans !

I do not call you with a song,
Nor summon you with tears.
But all my prayers to you belong
When dusk's sad hour appears.

An arrow struck with deadly aim,
And one of you fell low ;
And while he kissed me, one became
An ugly carrion-crow.

So be it. One day in the year,
When thaw the frozen streams,
In Catharine Park I stand and hear,
Where the clean water gleams,

A ripple of wide-spreading wings
On smooth blue spaces swell.
I know not who the window flings
Wide on my tomb-like cell.

(C. M. Bowra)

Maybe again the organ-music blaring
Will like first thunder of the spring arise ;
Look there behind your bride and see me staring
Across her shoulder with my half-shut eyes.

Seven days' love, seven dread years dissevered,
War, revolution, and a home struck low ;
Hands of the young with guiltless blood are covered,
Grey locks of hair on rosy temples grow.

Good-bye, fair friend, be happy ; all is over.
I give back your sweet pledges of before ;

But do not tell to your devoted lover
The raving words that I shall say no more, —

Because their poisoned fire will break asunder
Your blessèd, your delightful marriage-tie,
While I reign in my garden full of wonder,
In which the Muses sing and grasses sigh.

(C. M. Bowra)

You are always new and always hidden ;
More each day I yield to your desire.
But your love, hard-hearted friend, has bidden
Me to tests of iron and of fire.

You forbid my song, forbid my laughter,
Long ago you told me not to pray.
But I care not for what happens after
If from you I am not cast away.

From the earth and skies you would me sever ;
I live, and my songs have ceased to swell.
'Tis as if to my free soul for ever
You had shut both Paradise and Hell.

(C. M. Bowra)

Is our time worse than all the times that went before it,
Except that in the frenzy of its anxious grief
It touched the blackest of our sores and wished to cure it
But had no strength to bring relief ?

There, in the West, Earth's sun still shines serene and steady,
And in its setting glow the roofs are glittering ;
But here Death marks the houses with a cross already,
And calls the ravens on.   Ravens are on the wing.

(C. M. Bowra)

Now we know well how each can bear the shock,
 What each must do : nothing can break us.
The Hour of Courage peals from every clock,
 Courage will not forsake us.
It is not terrible for us to give
 Our blood beneath the murderous hail,
If we know you, O Russian speech, shall live,
 And the great Russian word not fail.

Shining and free it shall be said we gave
This to our children, and thus from bondage save
The centuries to come.

(V. DE S. PINTO)

NIKOLAI POLETAEV
(1888–   )

The Red Square

EVERYWHERE blood-red banners streaming
    In pale-blue heavens fiercely bright
The silver words upon them gleaming
    Shine in the sun's cold slanting light :

And everywhere are pale stern faces,
    Ranks moving with firm measured tread,
And up there in the boundless spaces
    Iron birds humming overhead.

No boasting here, no exultation,
    No empty laughter's mocking peal :
Only cold, fixed determination,
    Duty unbending, firm as steel.

(V. DE S. PINTO)

BORIS PASTERNAK
(1890–   )

SWUNG down from the fragrant branches
  That drank of such bliss in the night,
A raindrop, drunk with the thunder,
  Slipped from flower to flower in flight.

From flower to flower dripping,
  It slid over two, and stayed
On both, a great agate hanging,
  And sparkled, and was afraid.

Wind blowing over the meadowsweet
  May flatten and tease that drop ;
But the couple will not be parted
  Or from kissing and drinking stop.

They laugh, and they try to sever,
  Stand up and make a new start,
But the drop will not fall from their pistils, —
  Though you cut them, they will not part.

(C. M. BOWRA)

Do not Touch

" DON'T touch.   Fresh paint ", the notice said.
  Soul no attention paid,
And memory's in smears that cheeks,
  Legs, hands, lips, eyes have made.

More than for all good luck or bad
  I loved you just because
All in this white and yellow world
  Through you still whiter was.

And my own gloom, my friend, I swear,
  Shall whiter be somehow
Than fever, lampshade, or the white
  Bandage upon a brow.

(C. M. BOWRA)

Sparrow Hills

KISSES on the breast, like water from a pitcher !
Not always, not ceaseless spurts the summer's well.
Nor shall we raise up the hurdy-gurdy's clamour
Each night from the dust with feet that stamp and trail.

I have heard of age, — those hideous forebodings !
When no wave will lift its hands up to the stars.
If they speak, you doubt it. No face in the meadows,
No heart in the pools, and no god in the firs.

Rouse your soul to frenzy. Let to-day come foaming.
It's the world's midday. Have you no eyes for it ?
Look how in the heights thought sseethe into white bubbles
Of fir-cones, woodpeckers, clouds, pine-needles, heat.

Here the rails are ended of the city tram-cars.
Further, pines must do. Further, trams cannot pass.
Further, it is Sunday. Plucking down the branches,
Skipping through the clearings, slipping on the grass.

Sifting midday light and Whitsunday and walking
Woods would have us think the world is always so ;
They're so planned with thickets, so inspired with spaces,
Fallen from the clouds on us, like chintz below.

(C. M. BOWRA)

Summer

ATHIRST for insects, butterflies,
And stains we long had waited,
And round us both were memories
Of heat, mint, honey plaited.

No clocks chimed, but the flail rang clear
-From dawn to dusk and planted
Its dreams of stings into the air ;
The weather was enchanted.

Strolled sunset to its heart's content,
Then yielded to cicadas
And stars and trees its government
Of gardens and of larders.

The moon in absence, out of sight,
Not shade but baulks was throwing,
And softly, softly the shy night
From cloud to cloud was flowing.

From dream more than from roof, and more
Forgetful than faint-hearted,
Soft rain was shuffling at the door.
And smell of wine-corks spurted.

So smelt the dust.　So smelt the grass
And if we chanced to heed them,
Smell from the gentry's teaching was
Of brotherhood and freedom.

The councils met in villages ;
Weren't you with those that held them ?
Bright with wood-sorrel hung the days,
And smell of wine-corks filled them.

(C. M. BOWRA)

In the Wood

A LILAC heat was heavy on the meadow,
High in the wood cathedral's darkness swelled.
What in the world was left still for their kisses ?
It was all theirs, soft wax in fingers held.

Such is the dream — you do not sleep, but only
Dream that you thirst for sleep, that someone lies
Asleep, and through his dream beneath his eyelids
Two black suns sear the lashes of his eyes.

Rays flowed, and with the ebbing flowed the beetles ;
Upon his cheeks the dragon-flies' gloss stirs.
The wood was full of careful scintillations
As under pincers at the clockmaker's.

It seemed he slumbered to the tick of figures,
While in harsh amber high above they set
Their nicely tested clocks up in the ether
And regulate and move them to the heat.

They shift them round about, and shake the needles,
Scatter shadow, and swing, and bore a place
For darkness like a mast erected upward
In day's decline upon its blue clock-face.

It seems that ancient happiness flits over ;
It seems sleep's setting holds the woodland close.
Those who are happy do not watch clocks ticking,
But sleep, it seems, is all this couple does.

(C. M. BOWRA)

THE air is whipped by the frequent rain-drops ;
The ice is grey and mangy.   Ahead
You look for the skyline to awaken
And start ; you wait for the drone to spread.

As always, with overcoat unbuttoned,
With muffler about his chest undone,
He pursues before him the unsleeping
Silly birds and chases them on.

Now he comes to see you, and, dishevelled,
The dripping candles he tries to snuff,
Yawns and remembers that now's the moment
To take the hyacinths' night-caps off.

Out of his senses, ruffling his hair-mop,
Dark in his thoughts' confusion, he
Leaves you quite dumbfounded with a wicked
Stupid tale that he tells of me.

(C. M. BOWRA)

Spring

IT's spring, I leave a street where poplars are astonished,
Where distance is alarmed and the house fears it may fall,
Where air is blue just like the linen bundle
A discharged patient takes from hospital,

Where dusk is empty, like a broken tale,
Abandoned by a star, without conclusion,
So that expressionless, unfathomable,
A thousand clamouring eyes are in confusion.

(C. M. Bowra)

Spasskoye

UNFORGETTABLE September is strewn about Spasskoye.
Is to-day not the time to leave the cottage here?
Beyond the fence Echo has shouted with the herdsman,
And in the woods has made the axe's stroke ring clear.

Last night outside the park the chilling marshes shivered.
The moment the sun rose it disappeared again.
The hare-bells will not drink of the rheumatic dew-drops,
On birches dropsy swells a dirty lilac stain.

The wood is melancholy.   What it needs is quiet
Under the snows in bear-dens' unawaking sleep.
And there among the boles inside the blackened fences
Jaws of the columned park, like a long death-list, gape.

The birchwood has not ceased to blot and lose its colour,
To thin its watery shadows and grow sparse and dim.
He is still mumbling, — you're fifteen years old again now,
And now again, my child, what shall we do with them?

So many of them now that you should give up playing.
They're like birds in bushes, mushrooms along hedges.
Now with them we've begun to curtain our horizon
And with their mist to hide another's distances.

On his death-night the typhus-stricken clown hears tumult,
The gods' Homeric laughter from the gallery.
Now from the road, in Spasskoye, on the timbered cottage
Looks in hallucination the same agony.

(C. M. Bowra)

STARS raced headlong.   Seaward headlands lathered.
Salt spray blinded.   Eyes dried up their tears.
Darkness filled the bedrooms.   Thoughts raced headlong.
To Sahara Sphinx turned patient ears.

Candles guttered.   Blood, it seemed, was frozen
In the huge Colossus.   Lips at play
Swelled into the blue smile of the desert.
In that hour of ebb night sank away.

Seas were stirred by breezes from Morocco.
Simoom blew.   Archangel snored in snows.
Candles guttered.   First text of *The Prophet*
Dried, and on the Ganges dawn arose.

(C. M. Bowra)

January 1919

THAT year!   How often " Out you fall! "
The old year's whisper at my window said.
The new year makes an end of all
And brings a Dickens Christmas tale instead.

He murmurs : " Shake yourself, forget ".
Mercury rises with the sun outside,
Just as the old year strychnine set
And fell down in the glass from cyanide.

For by his hand and by his dawn
And by his hair that indolently stirs
Outside the window Peace is drawn
From birds and roofs as from philosophers.

Now here he comes, lies in the light
That shines from panels and from snow out there.
He's boisterous and impolite,
Shouts, calls for drink, — it is too much to bear.

He's off his head.   With him he brings
The hubbub of the yard.   What can you do ?
In all the world no sufferings
Are such that they will not be cured by snow.

(C. M. Bowra)

May it be

Dawn shakes the candle, shoots a flame
To light the wren and does not miss.
I search my memories and proclaim :
" May life be always fresh as this ! "

Like a shot dawn rang through the night,
Bang-bang it went.   In swooning flight
The wads of bullets flame and hiss.
May life be always fresh as this.

The breeze is at the door again.
At night he shivered, wanted us.
He froze when daybreak came with rain.
May life be always fresh as this.

He is astonishingly queer.
Why rudely past the gateman press ?
Of course he saw " No entrance here ".
May life be always fresh as this.

Still with a handkerchief to shake,
While mistress still, chase all about, —
While yet our darkness does not break,
While yet the flames have not gone out.

(C. M. Bowra)

So they begin.   With two years gone
From nurse to countless tunes they scuttle.
They chirp and whistle.   Then comes on
The third year, and they start to prattle.

So they begin to see and know.
In din of started turbines roaring
Mother seems not their mother now,
And you not you, and home is foreign.

What meaning has the menacing
Beauty beneath the lilac seated,
If to steal children's not the thing ?
So first they fear that they are cheated.

So ripen fears.   Can he endure
A star to beat him in successes,
When he's a Faust, a sorcerer ?
So first his gipsy life progresses.

So from the fence where home should lie
In flight above are found to hover
Seas unexpected as a sigh.
So first iambics they discover.

So summer nights fall down and pray
" Thy will be done " where oats are sprouting,
And menace with your eyes the day.
So with the sun they start disputing.

So verses start them on their way.

(C. M. Bowra)

We're few, perhaps not more than three,
Flaming, infernal, from the Don,
Beneath a sky racing and grey
Of rain, clouds, soldiers bent upon
Soviets, verses and long talk
Of transport and the artist's work.

Once we were men, we're epochs now,
Knocked, whirling in a caravan,
Like tundra 'neath the tender's sough,
While pistons, sleepers rattle on.
We'll join our flights, break through, make touch,
Spun round in ravens' eddying rush,

And on ! Later you'll understand.
So at dawn striking on piled straw,
Instantly hurling all around,
The wind becomes eternal where
Trees in a meeting's stormy din
Talk as a ruined house falls in.

(C. M. BOWRA)

Love is for some a heavy cross ;
Your beauty has got nothing twisted ;
Your charm to life's enigma is
The secret key, and I have guessed it.

In spring rustling is heard again,
And news and truths that ripple running.
Your race has sprung from such a strain ;
Like air, your mind is free from cunning.

Easy to wake, again to see,
To shape away heart's wordy litter,
Nor henceforth choked in life to be, —
No need for skill in such a matter.

(C. M. BOWRA)

If I had known what would come later,
When first my stage career began,
That words will take to blood and slaughter,
Go for the throat and kill a man,

To jest with such an ugly lining,
Point-blank refusal I'd have made, —

So far away was my beginning,
My first concern was so afraid.

But age is Rome, which, in impatience
Of jokes and acrobats, will cry
Not for an actor's recitations
But that in earnest he should die.

Feelings dictate a line and send it,
A slave upon the stage, and that
Means that the task of art is ended,
And there's a breath of earth and fate.

(C. M. BOWRA)

Summer Day

IN spring before the dawn we see
Heaps in the kitchen garden,
As pagans for fertility
Their festal altars burden.

The fresh-cut clods flame in my plot;
It steams at early morning,
And all the earth becomes red-hot
Just like an oven burning.

I cast aside this shirt of mine
Where my earth-labour takes me;
The heat strikes down upon my spine
And like wet clay it bakes me.

I stand up where the sun's rays beat;
With screwed-up eyes I burnish
Myself from head to foot with heat,
As with a fiery varnish.

Night, bursting on the corridor,
Comes to my sleeping quarter,
And leaves me brimming like a jar
With lilac and with water.

The upper layer she wipes away
From cooling walls, and laden
With me for gift she offers me
To any country maiden.

(C. M. BOWRA)

Spring 1944

THIS spring there is a change in everything.
More lively is the sparrows' riot.
I shall not even try to tell of it,
How bright my soul is and how quiet.

My thoughts and writings are quite different,
And from the choir's loud octaves singing
The mighty voice of earth is audible
Of liberated countries ringing.

The breath of spring across this land of ours
Wipes winter's marks from off its spaces
And washes off black rings that tears have made
Round red eyes of Slavonic faces.

The grass is waiting everywhere to burst,
And though in ancient Prague the alleys
Are silent, each more crooked than the rest,
They'll burst in song soon, like the gullies.

From Czech, Moravian and Serbian,
By the soft hands of spring uplifted;
Tales tear away the sheet of lawlessness
And burst with buds where snow has drifted.

All will be dim in mist of fairy-tales,
Like patterns on the wall that dazzle
In golden chambers where the Boyars lived
Or on the great church of St. Basil.

A dreamer and a thinker in the night,
Moscow is dearer than the world.   Her dower
Is to be home and source of everything
With which the centuries will flower.

(C. M. BOWRA)

ILYA EHRENBURG
(1891–   )

The Trumpet

I AM the trumpet blown by time ;
I have to call — they may believe.
But who will know the truth sublime
That even brass can weep and grieve ?

He forced my lips that had been dumb
To howl with prophecy and fright :
I made from boredom — martyrdom,
The tragic eve — from simple night.

He came — and no one could withstand.
What did they say ?   Whom did they call ?
So thousands roared throughout the land,
And Master Time — he blew them all.

It was not I who turned the pages
With steady hand and unafraid,
Presenting to the court of ages
Hordes of blind masons on parade.

I did not speak, I but replied ;
For, struck by Time, my mouth is torn,
For I am not the mighty tide,
But only Man, of woman born.

The trumpet lives.   But who can see
That by this brass, with blood imbued,
I glorify the victory
Of those by whom I was subdued ?

(Y. HORNSTEIN)

THE day will come : our sufferings will be
Nothing but dates inscribed by history,
And those in happy houses will not know
Of slaves who toiled in quarries long ago.

Yet, traces of past struggles will be found
Embedded in the womb of hardened ground, —
Not legends, stale, preserved from ancient times,
Nor staler verses and forgotten rhymes,
Nor furious Tables, forged in Sinai's brand, —
But just a hand that claps another hand,
So that the children of an easy life
Should know the victory we won in strife,
The victory of human heart and breath,
Not over man, but simply over death.

For all the raging tempests tried in vain
To part the fingers clasped in love and pain.
A sudden shot, the creaking of a door, —
The greatest loss was loss for us no more.
When children, on the graves we used to play,
Our love was strongest on our dying day, —
And death himself became a sacred myth,
The wistful smile of blessed Sulamaith.

(Y. HORNSTEIN)

BEHOLD, newcomer, liberty is dead.
New grievous Lourdes is part of your machine,
And miracles imbue the faultless tread
Of strictly measured hearts and stars unseen.

Thus, of the things that yesterday we loved
Remain the classics, and the rocky stone
On which the cloaked romantic stood and moved
His world of song, forgotten and alone.

Your giant cyclops, obstinate and grand,
Frowning his ageless frown, is marching on ;

He scans already, compasses in hand,
With envious eye, the tower of Babylon.

Forgive that I was born so long ago,
And love the days that now are loved no more,
The cooing pigeons in the Kremlin's snow,
And flickering lights through the cathedral's door.

Now you may crush me with a single turn
Of any of your wheels that throb and thud.
You spilled your sweat, and I shall spill my blood,
Yet still the heavens, pierced, will burst and burn.

(Y. Hornstein)

OSIP MANDELSTAM
(1892–1939)

Meganom

TRANSPARENT still in the far distance,
The spring of asphodels is grey;
And still, while with its old persistence
Rustles the sand, the waters play.
But here my soul will pass for ever
On light wheel like Persephone.
The Kingdom of the Dead will sever
The sunburnt hand so dear to me.

Why trusted to a boat reposes
The heavy urn that seeks the grave?
Why ends the feast of the black roses
Over the amethystine wave?
Thither my spirit hastens yearning
In mist beyond Cape Meganom,
And when the funeral's done, returning
The sable sail will travel home.

Beyond the unhallowed verge pass over
The clouds, and disappear, how soon!
Black companies of roses hover
And fly beneath the windy moon.
And, bird of death and lamentation,
With mourning edge, comes slowly nigh
Memory's flag in its proud station
Above the cypress stern on high.

And sadly, while the sands still quiver,
The perished years a fan unfold;
Where the descending shadows shiver,
The sandy dunes an amulet hold.
Thither my spirit hastens yearning
In mist beyond Cape Meganom,
And when the funeral's done, returning
The sable sail will travel home.

(C. M. BOWRA)

VLADIMIR MAYAKOVSKY
(1893–1930)

Listen

LISTEN !
Just because the stars light up their fires,
Does it mean that someone insists on it ?
Does it mean that they answer someone's desires ?
Does it mean that someone gives the name of pearls
    to that spit ?
And toiling and moiling
In storms of the midday heat
Does he force his way upon God ?
Does he fear he is late,
Lament,
And kiss God's sinewy hand
And demand
That a star be compelled to exist ?
Does he swear
That this starless torment he will not stand ?
After that
He goes about alarmed,
Though quiet to look at.
He says to someone :
" Is that nothing to you ?
Are you not afraid ?
True ? "
Listen !
Just because the stars
Light up their fires,
Does it mean that someone insists on it,
Does it mean that someone must have it so,
That every evening
Over the roofs
One star at least must be kindled and glow ?

(C. M. BOWRA)

Left March

FALL in and prepare to march !
No time now to talk or to trifle.
Silence, you orators !
The word
Is with you,
Comrade Rifle !
We have lived long enough by laws
Of which Adam and Eve made the draft.
Stable history's poor old horse !
Left !
Left !
Left !

Hallo, bluejackets !
Up in the tops !
Over the oceans !
Or
Have your battleships in the docks
Lost the edge that they had before ?
See,
Showing the teeth of its crown,
The British lion rebuffed.
The Commune will never go down.
Left !
Left !
Left !

Out there
Past fiery peaks advance
To a sunny land unknown.
Past hunger,
Past pestilence,
Let millions march on.
Though hirelings circle to crush us
And the lava of steel flow swift,
The Entente cannot conquer the Russias.
Left !
Left !
Left !

Does the eagle's eye grow dim
While on old haunts it lingers ?
Make fast
On the throat of the world
Proletarian fingers.
Fling chests out straight.
In the sky let the banners drift.
Who marches there with the right ?
Left !
Left !
Left !

(C. M. BOWRA)

GEORGE IVANOV
(1894–   )

Roses over against your window,
  Stars o'er the lonely garden gleam ;
Only blue clouds of incense rising,
  Only a dream within a dream.

Fresh and calm is the light around us,
  Cool from the depths that coolness bring ;
This it is in this world of ours,
  This it is that men call the Spring.

Joy wide-eyed, grief black and stricken,
  The fair fresh land and the twilit sky ;
This is what in this world of ours,
  This is what men call Destiny.

That of which no man guesses the meaning,
  That which of men shall never be known —
Only the warm sea makes her moan ;
Only the sails of the tall ship struggle
  Fighting the storm that the winds have sown.

(Maud F. Jerrold)

SERGEI ESENIN
(1895–1925)

Autumn

AUTUMN, chestnut mare, quietly stirs,
Cleans her mane upon the hillside junipers.

On the shore that holds the river's bounds
The blue clanging of her hoof-beats sounds.

Walks the monkish wind with wary tread
On the cluttered road where leaves lie dead ;

As he goes, he kisses on a rowan-tree
Red wounds gaping in a Christ he cannot see.

(C. M. BOWRA)

Song about a Bitch

AT dawn in her kennel of rye-stalks,
On the golden rushes there,
A bitch had a litter of puppies,
Seven puppies with red-brown hair.

She fondled them till the evening
And licked them, until the snow
Beneath the warmth of her belly
Half thawed and began to flow.

But when the hens in the evening
To their perches fluttered back,
The grim master came and bundled
The seven pups into a sack.

After him over the snow-drifts
She ran and kept up with his pace,
And long, ah long, did she shudder
At the pond's flat unfrozen face.

But when she came back to her kennel
And licked sweat away from her side,
She thought the moon over the cottage
Was one of the pups who had died.

She gazed in the dark-blue vastness,
And her whining was loud and shrill,
But the flimsy moon slid onward
And hid in the fields by a hill.

And dumbly, as if she were smitten
By men in jest with a stone,
The eyes of the bitch like golden
Stars in the snowdrift shone.

(C. M. Bowra)

I am the last village-poet,
A plain plank-bridge of songs am I ;
While leaves of the birch scatter incense,
I stand for my poor good-bye.

Low from the wax of the body
In golden flames sinks the light,
And moons, the clocks of the village,
Will rattle out my midnight.

Soon by the blue path in the meadow
The iron guest comes on his way,
And with swarthy hand he will gather
The oat-stalk spilt by the day.

O hands unfamiliar and lifeless,
My songs cannot live with you.
Only ears of corn like horses
Will mourn for the master they knew.

The wind will suck the sad whinny
And dance at the funeral rite.
Soon, soon the clocks of the village
Will rattle out my midnight.

(C. M. Bowra)

THE little thatched house I was born in
   Is bare to the sky,
And in these crooked alleys of Moscow
   I am fated to die.

No hope have I now of returning
   To the fields where I played,
Of hearing the song of the poplars
   As I lie in the shade.

The city is senile and dingy and drab,
   But I love it.
The golden and somnolent East
   Lies brooding above it.

And at night when the moon is a-shining,
   (A hell of a moon)
I lurch through the slum till I come
   To my favourite saloon.

There all the night through there is riot,
   And babble and sin.
I read out my verses to harlots
   And treat them to gin.

Still faster and fiercer my heart beats :
   This is all I can say :
" I am lost, you are lost, we are all lost,
   I don't know the way."

The little thatched house I was born in
   Is bare to the sky,
And in these crooked alleys of Moscow
   I am fated to die.

(R. M. HEWITT)

Last Lines

Now good-bye, my friend, good-bye, my darling.
In my heart I keep you safe with me.
Our predestined parting gives a promise
Of a meeting in the time to be.

Now good-bye, my friend, no hand clasped, no word spoken.
Do not let me vex or sadden you.
In this life there's nothing new in dying,
And, in truth, to live is nothing new.

(C. M. BOWRA)

NIKOLAI TIKHONOV
(1896–   )

I WAS born at night on the crossways,
And at my first breath earth's cry
Came to my ears long and jarring,
As the cranes call when they fly.

I lived like a path by a fir-tree
Where wheels rattle all day through.
A freezing cat at my cradle
Would warm its paws and mew.

There came to me waters and countries
Of birch-woods with birds at play ;
My father did not tell me my future
Nor look down where I lay.

(C. M. Bowra)

WE have unlearned to give when beggars cry,
To breathe the air on heights where salt seas splash,
To greet the sunrise or on stalls to buy
The gold of lemons for our copper trash.

By accident boats reach us now and then,
And rails from habit their old burdens bear.
Count up the number of my countrymen ;
How many dead will at the roll appear ?

We pass triumphant and disdainful hours.
For work a broken knife is useless, but
With these same black and broken knives of ours
Pages that live for ever have been cut.

(C. M. Bowra)

NOT yesterday did the blacksmith hammer
My soul; ice for long kept it cold.
" Give your hand to me," came the night hill's clamour,
" I shall follow wherever I'm told."

When days of sunshine to cross-roads brought me,
Sign-posts had a golden glow.
The bridges fell at my feet and besought me
That over them I should go.

And the woods cried out : " We wait for the power
Of your faithful axes to come."
The hills and ravines in a flaming shower
Kept me warm in a secret home.

And I was dissolute, I was drunken,
For blood, like a lynx, still athirst,
And by stony suns all my frame was shrunken, —
But my lips into song's flame burst.

(C. M. BOWRA)

A FIRE, a hawser, bullets and an axe,
Like lackeys greeted us, and followed after.
In every drop a deluge slept,
Through little stones hills sprang into existence,
And in a briar trampled underfoot
Loud was the sound of forests with black arms.

With us untruth partook of food and drink,
Bells rang their changes in the usual manner,
Coins lost their weight and lost their ringing sound,
And children were not startled by dead bodies.
And in that time we were the first to learn
To use words bitter, beautiful and cruel.

(C. M. BOWRA)

THE enemy has forced an entry
Into our land of morning light. —
With bullets learn to stand on sentry,
Trust in your rifle, friend, and fight.

Our life was rich ; and envy-ridden
Foes coveted what we had got. —
Trust the grenade in your belt hidden,
Trust the sharp silver bullet's shot.

We shall come back to work, returning
With steps that march in liberty. —
Study war's tasks, like soldiers learning
To use your arms with mastery.

Let not the coward hope for pardon,
Let courage in the fight grow strong,
Let songs with vengeance for their burden
Take place of every other song.

(C. M. BOWRA)

EDUARD BAGRITSKY
(1896–1934)

The Fowler

HARD it is to be a fowler.
He must learn by heart the birds' names,
Times of flight he must remember,
Blow on whistles various.

But along the roadways stumbling,
Passing nights beneath the hedges,
Didel is quite happy, Didel
Sings his songs and catches birds.

In the grey, globed elder-bushes
Nightingales strike up their piping,
Tom-tits hang along the pine-trees,
Chaffinch flutters on the birch.

And then Didel fishes softly
Out of his forbidden wallet
Three decoy-pipes, dedicating
To each bird a different pipe.

First, he blows a pipe of elder,
And the pipe of elder tinkles.
From the screen of elder bushes
Answers back the nightingale.

Then he blows a pipe of pine-wood,
Whistles on his pipe of pine-wood.
From the pine-trees tom-tits answer,
Scattering their tambourines.

And then Didel fishes softly
Out of his forbidden wallet
His most light and his most ringing
Pipe that is of birch-wood made.

141

He tries out the concords gently,
Blows into the holes for music,
With the birch-tree's voice sonorous
Underneath his breath he sings.

And when to that voice it listens,
Voice of birds and voice of woodlands,
On the birch-tree by the wayside
Chaffinch thunders back reply.

Then, beyond the country roadway,
Where the rumbling cart is silent,
By the ponds that duckweed covers
Didel spreads his meshes out.

And around, with green below it,
And with grey and blue above it,
An enormous bird-world rises,
Whistles, clicks, and jingles there.

So on Didel travels, happy,
With his stick and birds and wallet,
Through the Hartz o'ergrown with forests
To the banks of river Rhine,

Through the great Thuringian oak-woods,
Through the Saxon woods of pine-trees,
Through Westphalian elder-bushes,
Through Bavarian drunkenness.

Martha, must you weep if Didel
Travels through the country places,
If he calls the birds with whistles,
Bursts in unexpected laughs ?

(C. M. BOWRA)

A PIECE of black bread and a faithful wife
With sickness and poverty poison life. . . .

The years that were tested by hoof-beat and stone,
The streams that in deathless floods have flown,
And wormwood that burned on our lips like flame. . . .
For us knives are too tame,
Pens are no good to us,
Picks do not please,
And glory's not glorious.
We are rusty leaves
On rusty oak-trees. . . .
Come the wind,
Come the cold,
And we fly away.
For whose approach is the carpet we lay ?
Whose feet will pass over us worn and wan ?
Will the young trumpeters over us tread ?
Will strange constellations rise overhead ?
We are rusted oaks whose peace has gone . . .
Shivering, homeless, we drive peace away. . . .
Into night we fly !
Into night we fly !
Like ripe stars, we fly anywhere. . . .
Over us the young trumpeters sound their peal,
Over us the strange constellations wheel,
Over us strange banners flap in the air. . . .
Come the wind,
Come the cold, —
We hurry after them,
We follow after them,
We whirl after them,
On the steppe our songs sound,
In the clouds after the bayonet's gleam,
After the hoof where the bear-dens dream,
And the trumpet's song, till in woods they are drowned.

(C. M. BOWRA)

VISSARION SAYANOV
(–)

The Voice

MIRRORED in distant lakes, and gleaming
Where rowing-boats and barges go,
Where birds above the pool are dreaming,
There is a star with greenish glow.

Trees wither, overgrown with mosses,
Beyond where the rough heath is grey.
Tall wood-piles smoke, and slowly passes
The wormwood-tasting smoke away.

Out there the shadows are declining
Where a low bank the river holds ;
And there barefooted girls are twining
Bright garlands of white marigolds.

A hundred stars, — the sun has broken
Into a hundred sparks that glow
With gold, and a slow voice has woken
To sing of days dead long ago.

It sings of how the heart is brimming
With sorrow for some old mischance, —
But on the stream a boat is swimming,
And sails upon the current dance.

— My home, with blossoms decked around you,
Set in a land of glorious name,
Where woods and spreading fields surround you,
I hear that voice still, just the same !

The sleigh creaks, while through snow it passes,
But in my mind those boats stay yet ;
Never can I those barefoot lasses,
Never that innocent voice forget !

(C. M. BOWRA)

GEORG SANNIKOV
(1899–   )

In Spring

It's spring.   The gentle breezes rustle;
Above the town the loud rooks cry.
How tired in the shop's noise and bustle
Are weavers when the dusk is nigh.

And I am tired from weaving, weaving;
Now is the hour for home, for home. . . .
With strange hid love for it I'm leaving
My bench until the morning come.

I go, and by the road unfrozen
The streamlets to the evening sing;
And my tired memory has chosen
A song of weaving in the spring.

Far sights my eyes are finding, finding;
Slaking their thirst the blue sky flows;
And the delighted eve is winding
Her threads of azure and of rose.

(C. M. Bowra)

MIKHAIL ISAKOVSKY
(1900–   )

Two girls of Ukraine,
Two lasses were singing,
One morning in Autumn,
When wild geese were winging.

Two geese said good-bye
To their nestlings upgrowing,
To the streams and the fields
Where the Dnieper is flowing.

The wild geese were crying
In the clear sky above :
" There's nothing more dear
Than the land that we love ".

The wild geese fly away,
Now fades summer weather,
It's time in the forest
Ripe bilberries to gather.

The hazels bow down
To the earth as in mourning,
The nuts from the boughs
In showers are falling.

The lasses walk on
Through the woods side by side ;
Above them the heavens
Stretch stormy and wide.

The poplars are ravaged,
The maples are torn,
In a wild rout the leaves
Through the forest are borne.

And the paths are all strewn
With gold drift far and near :

Sad music and tender
Those lasses would hear.

Suddenly from the sky
The geese call again,
They sing of sad partings,
Of sorrow and pain.

They cry as above
The dark wood they wing,
Two feathers for memory
To the lasses they fling.

And the girls stand and nod
Their two little heads,
Just like two young rowans
In wild woodland glades.

They sing a farewell
To the wild geese above :
" There's nothing so dear
As the land which we love ".

(V. DE S. PINTO)

STEPAN SHCHIPACHEV
(1899–   )

Snowflake

IT's four o'clock, and I shan't sleep till morning.
The snow-storm thickens, night flies on to day.
Earth, as if wound with clock-work, goes on turning. . . .
Hundreds, thousands of years will pass away
Till that far age we dream of in the distance
Comes trumpeting with storms like those we see,
And in it far beyond our thought's persistence,
A snowflake, yes, just that, is what I'd be,
In flight above the earth in stormy weather,
To glance just once upon the coming years,
And flutter on a poplar, like a feather,
Till on a young girl's cheek it disappears.

(C. M. BOWRA)

SHE used to rock the cradle.   They would leave her
To watch her baby brother all the day.
The sunflowers would nod behind the paling
With heads like red-haired youngsters at their play.

She grew.   She used to carry cattle-fodder,
Climbing up stacks of straw she used to go,
She lay unconscious, sick with scarlet fever,
She fell down with her buckets in the snow.

The neighbour's bull would shake his monstrous forehead,
Threaten to charge, brandish his horns at her.
What danger did not menace her in childhood?
Of that small child I would have taken care.

Maybe my strength that comes from peasant fathers
Still slept beneath time's load and did not stir,
And maybe I was not as yet begotten,
But that small child carried my life in her.

(C. M. BOWRA)

ALEXANDER KOVALENKOV
(-   )

Be near me

DEAREST, in that world so far away,
Think of me a little while to-day.

Think of me with love, unswerving, true —
But you must not call me back to you.

Never, darling, bid me to return :
Never bow your head and never mourn.

Let not Sorrow come to cast his grey
Shadow on your eyes this bright spring day,

This spring day when, breaking ice, we tramp
Through the rust-red marshes' endless damp,

Through the roads awash with heavy rains,
Through Karelia's wet and woody lanes.

At this hour when mines go up and shroud
Far blue valleys with a smoky cloud,

And the shells whirl by in screaming flight,
Burst and burn the birches' silver white,

At this hour when fire fills earth and sky,
O be near me, to my spirit fly,

That my faith may grow more strong, more pure
Be my strength, my courage to endure.

(V. DE S. PINTO)

KONSTANTIN SIMONOV
(1915–   )

" *Tears cost her nothing anyway* "

BORN beautiful, I hear them say,
You'll have good fortune all the way.

Poor child, misfortune, suffering, praying
   Your death itself will be in vain,
You'll not defeat that foolish saying,
   The cunning comfort of the plain.
They'll say you snatch by beauty's art
All that is yours by warmth of heart.

Be tender, faithful, what you will,
   But still the same old tale is told,
The beautiful are heartless still,
   The fortunate are always cold.
They'll hear what love is poured on you,
That only shows what looks can do !

Perhaps you'll marry out of guile,
   Still, still to beauty love's denied,
They'll credit you with all that's vile,
   The lust and greed that they must hide.
With pride your husband you adore ?
Because you need him, nothing more !

Your husband dies : his faults are spared,
   But still on you their verdict's damning.
Forget him — then you never cared,
   Or don't forget — and then you're shamming.
And let her cry, you'll hear them say,
Tears cost her nothing anyway !

Yet quiet pain wins no belief
   Nor hidden tears.   They do not care
That when a child, unchildish grief
   Befell you in the market-square.
You suffered wounds too deep to heal ?
The beautiful can scarcely feel !

I was not angry when of late
  You scorned me too with unbelief,
The beautiful and fortunate
  Can only trust in loss and grief.
Oh, if you'd known this all ahead
Your beauty would have withered dead.

You'll reach perhaps felicity,
  Or pine from gnawing pain within,
Or live, uncomforted by me,
  But the unholy saw will win : —
Born beautiful, I hear them cry,
You're fortunate until you die !

(FRANCES CORNFORD)

WAIT, and I'll be home again,
  Only wait for me. . . .
Wait although the yellow rain
  Patters dismally,
Wait in snowstorm's sweeping blast,
  Wait in summer's heat,
Wait when, faithless to the past,
  Others do not wait.
Wait when from lands far away
  Letters never come,
Wait when all are bored who stay
  With you safe at home.

Wait, and I'll be home again.
  Heed them not who say
That all memory is vain
  Of the lost to-day.
Though my son and mother fret
  That I shan't return,
Though friends tired of waiting sit
  Where the fire-logs burn,
While the wine of grief they taste
  To my memory,
Wait a little, and do not haste
  To pledge yours to me.

Wait, and I'll be home again
In despite of doom.
Those who will not wait may feign
That luck brought me home.
How can those who would not wait
Understand or know
How your waiting kept my fate
Safe through war's red glow ?
Why I live, — that only we
Know, just I and you.
You knew how to wait for me
As none other knew.

(C. M. Bowra)

NOTES

p. 17. *A Prologue*, written for the second edition of the narrative poem, *Ruslan and Lyudmila*, in 1928. The characters mentioned are the familiar figures of Russian folk-lore.

p. 18. *Gipsy's Song*, sung by Zemphira in *The Gipsies*.

p. 21. *Monastery on Kasbek*, written in 1829 when Pushkin was with the Russian Army, then fighting against the Turks in Armenia.

p. 22. *Song in Time of Plague*, from the short play, *The City of the Plague*.

p. 27. Odoevsky was exiled to Siberia in 1826 for his part in the Decembrist revolt, and this poem was written from there.

p. 29. *O Liberty*. This used to be attributed to Ryleev, but there is no doubt that it is by Yazykov.

p. 66. *Evening mist* . . . The winged angel from the Koran was probably inspired by Edgar Allan Poe's poem, *Israfel*.

p. 70. *Ravenna*. Both Galla Placidia, mother of the Emperor Honorius, and Theodoric are buried at Ravenna. The "New Life" is a reference to the *Vita Nuova* of Dante, who is also buried there.

p. 76. *The Twelve*, written in January 1918.

p. 97. (ll. 8-9), probably intended to be cat language. Khlebnikov began as a Futurist who experimented with "trans-sense", that is, sounds without meaning.

p. 114. Written in 1941.

p. 119. *Stars raced headlong*. The poem is concerned with Pushkin's composition of his famous poem, *The Prophet*.

p. 131. *Left March*, written in 1918.

p. 136. The first verse of this poem is omitted in the translation.

p. 137. *Last Lines*, written by Esenin in his own blood before he hanged himself in the Hotel d'Angleterre in Leningrad.

p. 140. Written in 1941.

INDEX OF AUTHORS

THE END

PRINTED BY R. & R. CLARK, LTD., EDINBURGH